ELI BORNSTEIN

ELI BORNSTEIN

ARCTIC JOURNALS 1986 AND 1987

INTRODUCTION BY
ROALD NASGAARD

Figure.1
Vancouver / Toronto / Berkeley

22 23 24 25 26 5 4 3 2 1

Cataloguing data is available from Library and Archives Canada
ISBN 978-1-77327-175-0 (hbk.)

Design by Teresa Bubela
Editing by Steve Cameron
Copy editing by David Marsh
Proofreading by Alison Strobel
Measurements of artworks are given as height × width × depth
Cover image: *Hexaplane Structurist Relief No. 2* (*Arctic Series*), 1995–1998. Homage to Murray Adaskin. Acrylic enamel on aluminum and Plexiglas, 67.2 × 182.2 × 15.9 cm. University of Saskatchewan Art Collection: Gift of Dorothea Adaskin. Photograph by Troy Mamer.

Printed and bound in Canada by Friesens
Distributed internationally by Publishers Group West

Efforts have been made to determine all photography credits. The publisher apologizes for any omissions and would be grateful if notified for future printings.

Figure 1 Publishing Inc.
Vancouver BC Canada
www.figure1publishing.com

Figure 1 Publishing works in the traditional, unceded territory of the xʷməθkʷəy̓əm (Musqueam), Sḵwx̱wú7mesh (Squamish), and səlilwətaɬ (Tsleil-Waututh) peoples.

THE AUTHORS GRATEFULLY ACKNOWLEDGE SUPPORT FROM
The Saskatchewan Arts Board, through its Access Copyright Foundation Grant, Micro-Grant and Independent Artists Grant; the University of Saskatchewan, through the President's Office and University Library donors and, very generously, the Fleck Family Foundation, and Georgina Steinsky, Toronto.

For Christina and our daughters, Sarah and Thea

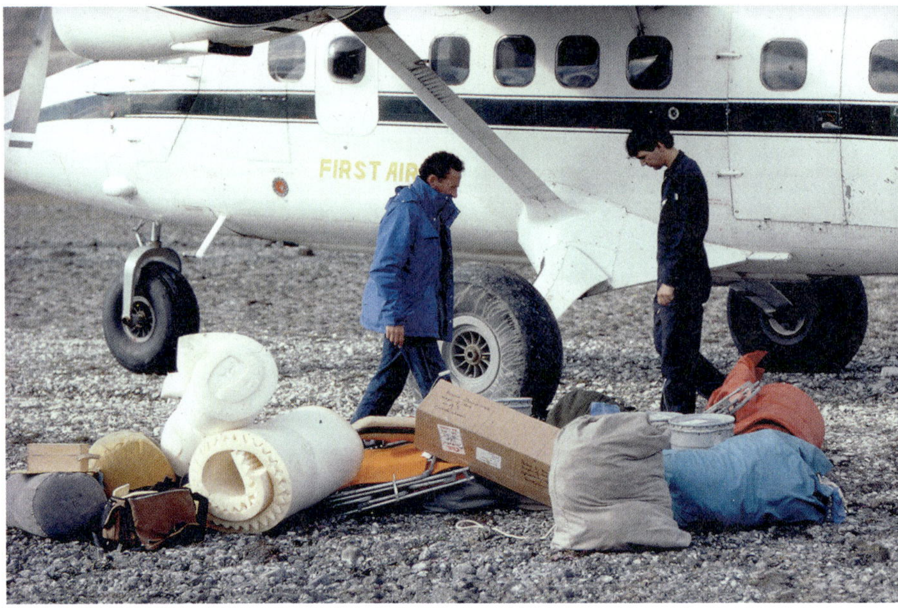

HANS DOMMASCH, **Unloading the Twin Otter** | 1986

Contents

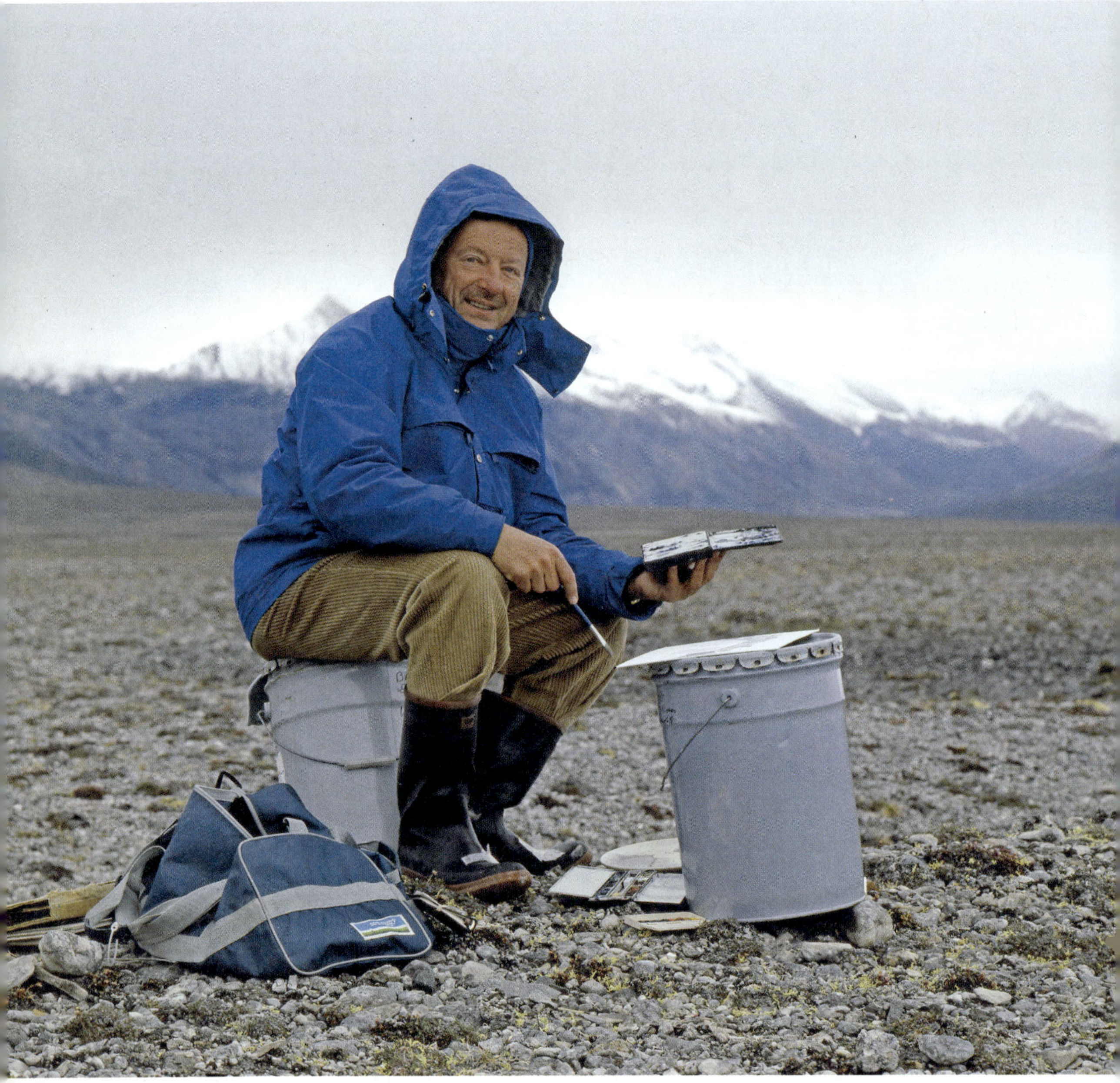

HANS DOMMASCH, **Eli Painting, Ellesmere Island** | 1986

Introduction: "A Very Sacred Experience"

ROALD NASGAARD

ELI BORNSTEIN HAD been north once before. In May 1965, he spent some ten days in Rankin Inlet in the company of two University of Saskatchewan colleagues, the musician/composer Murray Adaskin and the anthropologist, activist and politician Bob Williamson.[1] Bornstein was then a professor and head of the Department of Art and Art History, Adaskin was the head of the Department of Music, and Williamson had just joined the Department of Anthropology and was an associate director with the University's Institute for Northern Studies.

Williamson was also their local guide. Born in Britain, he had immigrated to Canada in 1952 and soon found himself living on Baffin Island where he learned to speak Inuktitut and, in 1959, founded the first Inuit language cultural journal, *Inuktitut*. Williamson had also worked with the Department of Northern Affairs, and in the 1960s served two terms as a member of the Legislative Council for the Northwest Territories.[2] Williamson owned a house in Rankin Inlet, which became the base of operations from which the three scouted out the region by foot, dogsled and skidoo. As Bornstein recalls, Williamson, who had adopted several Inuit children, was fully integrated into local life, allowing their stay to include close contact with the local Indigenous families. Bornstein also remembers how the three of them talked about collaborating on an opera set in the North, and how Adaskin recorded Inuit songs, including examples of throat singing, research that would figure in his future compositions.

The Rankin Inlet expedition, however seriously it was undertaken, was more about "exploring" things, Bornstein says. In contrast, the trips to Ellesmere Island in 1986 and 1987 with his travel companion, the photographer Hans Dommasch, were from the start purposed and single-mindedly dedicated to making art. Dommasch tells of how Bornstein had "for many years relentlessly explored the possibility of investigating the Canadian Arctic."[3]

And Bornstein himself, having flown out of Saskatoon airport the afternoon of July 23, 1986, mulls over this compulsion immediately in his first journal entry: "Not sure why, exactly, but [a] strong feeling of it being very important. As if it is to be a turning point in my life where thereafter all things will be reckoned as B.E. or A.E.—Before Ellesmere or After!" (ARCTIC JOURNALS, 23.VII.86). Dommasch, then head of the Department of Art and Art History at the University of Saskatchewan, who in 1986 also published his photographic celebration of the prairie grain elevator, *Prairie Giants*, came north with his own artistic objectives, but in the process documented moments of their travels and of their subsistence isolation out on the tundra.

Bornstein and Dommasch's Ellesmere trips were financed by a grant from the Polar Continental Shelf Project (PCSP), an agency of the Government of Canada.[4] PCSP also provided the logistical support to get a couple of "greenhorn" artists, as Dommasch dubbed the two of them, to their remote locations—along with food, tents, art supplies and whatever else they needed to be self-sufficient for longer periods of time in relative isolation—and to get them out again.

On crucial practical details, like food and supplies, it was fellow University of Saskatchewan professor James F. Basinger who provided them with experienced advice. Although Basinger was younger than both Bornstein and Dommasch, he was a seasoned Arctic explorer, and as Dommasch describes him, "a man of action." The PCSP had been set up in 1958 to facilitate the work of researchers in the Arctic, such as the work Basinger was undertaking in the Axel Heiberg Island fossil forest. Artists could be included in such projects by attaching them to scientific field parties when there was spare capacity. They could thus safely travel to otherwise inaccessible regions. Bornstein and Dommasch accompanied

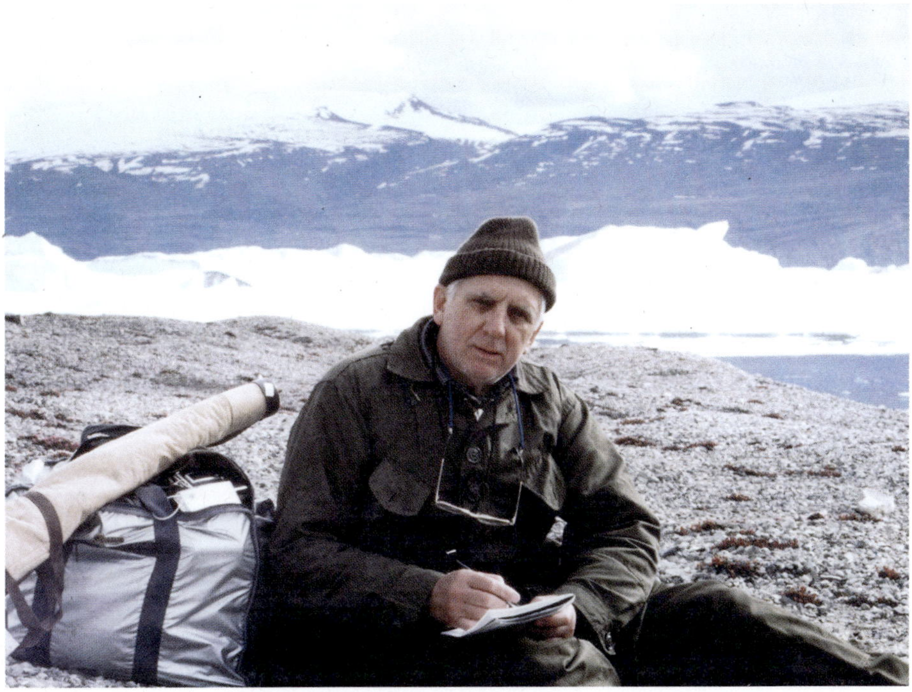

HANS DOMMASCH, **Self-Portrait, Otto Fjord** | 1986

Basinger and his team to Axel Heiberg on this basis in 1987, though in preparation for the 1986 trip they had already been personally interviewed by the director of the PCSP and were found trustworthy enough to be turned loose on their own on Ellesmere Island, although always under radio supervision.[5]

Perhaps their true logistics hero was Barry Hough, the base manager for PCSP stationed at Resolute Bay. They met him when they first flew in from Yellowknife in 1986. Hough would be their air transport coordinator and their general lifeline, as he was for all the other researchers and travellers strewn across the Arctic, many of whom Bornstein would meet as their respective paths crisscrossed on their way to far-flung destinations and back again. There were scheduled flights, usually on De Havilland Twin Otters, and unscheduled ones on which, when there were spare seats on a plane, Bornstein and Dommasch were invited along.

It was while living on Alexandra Fjord during his second summer visit that Bornstein had his first helicopter ride. Sitting in the front seat of the Plexiglas bubble, he was flown out over the icebergs on the easterly edge of Ellesmere Island, with Greenland not far across the water. Once the expedition even landed on an iceberg and dropped down onto an ice floe. At other times there were long hours of waiting for radio contact, waiting for the weather to change, or waiting for delayed, rerouted or postponed flights.

A mandatory routine for all travellers under PCSP jurisdiction was to maintain daily radio contact morning and evening with headquarters in Resolute Bay. Hough called these communications "the skids"—radio calls he had with each of the camps and groups from all over the world that were scattered across the Arctic.

In the morning of his first full day on Otto Fjord, Bornstein reports being up at 6:45 AM "to make our regular radio contact at 7 AM (two required daily—7 AM and 7 PM. XMH 26 is our call number)." On that evening's call when Bornstein asks Hough how things were back in Resolute, Hough replies exasperatedly that he is "fighting alligators." As Bornstein sympathizes in his journal entries, "He has a tough job requiring 17-hour days, babysitting all the groups and coordinating air travel, fuel, etc. No wonder he has developed such a grim sense of humour" (26.VII.86). On yet another evening, Bornstein, calling in from his own lonesome location, complains how a regular "skid" can take much too much time when there is a lot of radio traffic: "It can last over an hour and one listens to all manner of conversations ranging from instructions for operating equipment to orders for machinery parts to grocery lists and personal messages" from all the many parties scattered out there. Even so, he was indebted to those "incredible little radios" that, along with the airplanes, were their lifelines. The sound of the human voice and "the solitary drone of a distant approaching aircraft" heard in the silence of their remoteness "had profound significance" (15.VII.87).

BORNSTEIN WAS IN HIS 60S when he made his two summer visits to the Arctic. Extraordinary as they were, trips like these were also intrinsic to his regular working schedule. Falls and winters of the academic years were for teaching, while summers and sabbaticals were set aside for his art, working at home in the studio or getting out on the road for study and research. His destinations in North America over previous years ranged from Big Sur in California to the coast of Maine and to Algonquin Park in Ontario. Long before that, on sabbatical in 1957, he had taken a decisive trip through Europe to meet up with the major Constructivist relief artists then working in France, the Netherlands and Britain. This was when he built his own first geometric reliefs.

Bornstein was born in 1922 in Milwaukee, Wisconsin. He accepted a teaching job at the University of Saskatchewan in Saskatoon in 1950 while still completing his MSc in Fine Art at the University of Wisconsin–Madison. At the University of Saskatchewan he served as an influential teacher and a key actor in the growth and development of the art department until he retired in 1990. From his base in Saskatoon he has exhibited and been collected nationally and internationally and has received significant public art commissions. He is also a writer, editor and publisher who in 1960 inaugurated the internationally circulated periodical *The Structurist*, published out of the University of Saskatchewan. In it he drew from a distinguished international roster of writers to address the future of art and architecture, not in isolation, but within the larger context of subjects ranging from science and technology to culture, education and music. The periodical, whose last issue came out in 2020, also reflected Bornstein's ongoing commitment to issues of social justice and environmentalism.

Since his student years, Bornstein has understood his art as the evolutionary outcome of his systematic study of Modernist art through Impressionism, the Post-Impressionism of Georges Seurat and Paul Cézanne, into Cubism and Constructivism, and onwards into the abstraction of Piet Mondrian and his De Stijl colleagues. It was, however, in his analysis of Mondrian's work—when Mondrian, around 1918, opted for pure idealized abstraction—that Bornstein objected, refusing (along with his American colleague Charles Biederman) to turn his back on the vitality and complexity of nature. He would continue to use Mondrian's abstract vocabulary, his rectilinear structures, his hard-edge geometry and his flat planes of colour. But he would reject Mondrian's reductive primaries and embrace colour in all its plenitudinous hues. These he would deploy in three-dimensional relief elements extended from a ground plane into real space and revealed by the motility of light. Bornstein made it his challenge to look intensely at nature's life, its colours, forms, spaces and light, and to translate his findings into the dynamic formal language of his Structurist relief constructions. As he wrote in *The Structurist*, his reliefs propose not to imitate nature, but to reinvent it, so that "the otherwise mechanical, technological aspect of the constructed relief can be transcended," and transformed "into the warmth of human expression."[6]

Of course, one could not make reliefs living out of a tent out on the Arctic tundra. There was no workshop and no tools as there had been when he travelled in Europe in 1957, or even in Algonquin Park in 1964. In any case, their making was too complex and involved and, as he wrote, "often occupied me for several years or more" (16.VII.87). Instead, the tangible outcomes of the two summers spent on Ellesmere Island were his daily journal and the many drawings and watercolours he executed out in the landscape. The journals would end up running to nearly 24,000 words, and the on-site work would, once back in the Saskatoon studio, spawn more watercolour paintings and the iridescent group of Structurist reliefs that came to constitute his Arctic Series. In the pages of his journals—often written on the fly as he crouched in the shelter of his tent, then tidied up and given style once back home—he describes the day-to-day to-do of getting about, of painting in wind and weather and mosquitoes. He tells of encounters with the RCMP, with a range of Canadian and international research scientists, and with other travellers that crossed his path. He reflects profoundly on larger human issues of aesthetics and transcendence. But most eloquently he evokes the challenges of getting down on paper his observations of nature. From the grandest of glaciers and icebergs to the tiniest Arctic flowers, mosses and lichens, Bornstein's charge was to render what he saw not realistically—Dommasch's camera was already "doing that marvellously"—but analogously, in the terms of his own long-developed visual syntax (26.VII.86).

The first stay in 1986 ran some ten days and the second, in 1987, about three weeks. The latter began with a short but unique excursion to Axel Heiberg Island with Basinger, who was a professor of geological sciences, to visit the remains of an extraordinary, 45-million-year-old Eocene epoch fossil forest that he and his colleagues only the year before had begun to investigate systematically. Otherwise, Bornstein and Dommasch mostly spent their time in relative isolation on Ellesmere; Bornstein desired to be in lone communion with northern nature. He wrote often of being taken aback, whether by a sense of his human puniness against the vast scale of the icebergs and the barren mountains, or by the tiny brevity of human time set against the eternity of geological time. These were profoundly sublime experiences that Bornstein occasionally contextualizes within the North American Transcendentalist tradition with which he had long identified. They were also consequential for the evolution of his work with Structurist reliefs, quieting them, slowing them down and deepening their meditative intensity. They bode, as it were, a truly "A.E.—After Ellesmere" transformation in Bornstein's work, expressed not only in the Arctic Series reliefs but in the A.E. transcendent multiplane reliefs that he would, over the following decades, conjure forth from his nature observations along the banks of the South Saskatchewan River behind his home outside Saskatoon.[7]

Out on the tundra, making watercolours was not always easy going. On the very first day on Otto Fjord, about to set out on a hike to look for places to work, he upbraids himself for having forgotten to bring some useful painting things: a jar for water, a backpack and a folding stool (26.VII.86). Then there are the inevitable mishaps like on an early Sunday morning of the next year when, having reached his favourite working site, he unpacks his painting materials—some 35 pounds of weight—and the shoulder strap on his new paint box breaks. The box hits the rocks hard enough that the wood splinters and one of the hinges on the cover breaks. "The mosquitoes next join the fracas," he recalls, "and my new folding stool sinks in the sediment!" (12.VII.87) There are long days of treks across vast spaces, the goal always further off than it seems. Sometimes it rains or snows, and it's damp and shiveringly cold when he crouches down to work.

It's frustrating trying to catch the subject when the light continues to change and the icebergs move.

Nevertheless, back on that first day in 1986 he packs what paper, paint and brushes will fit into his "little blue bag," and sets off "to look" and paint his first subject. Despite mishaps and discomforts, watercolours get painted because there is always the magic of the light, the colour and the space, which is of a "scope beyond full human comprehension." You can fly over a terrain to get an overview, but that is no substitute for walking it to get sensory contact with its reality and to establish a "prolonged intimate encounter" with it. "One only gets to know a place by staying there" (18.vii.87). Surely, he concludes midway through the first summer, "there could be no better place for an artist to learn from nature about the possibilities of art than the Arctic. Here I am at 63 in this ultimate kindergarten!" (28.vii.86)

HIS IMMEDIATE CHALLENGE is to translate onto paper his impressions of the topography of the Arctic landscape, from the tiny delicacy of the Arctic flowers to the majesty of the icebergs seen in the ever-changing light of the 24-hour day. ("What," he wonders, "would Monet have made of these ice-stacks and mountain-cathedrals?" [26.vii.86]) I have "many paintings in my head," he reports, "beautiful" ones, but the challenge is how "to put colour down in a uniquely abstract way that evokes sensations without imitating appearances"—the camera, we remember, already accomplishes that—and which "has a life of its own yet bears some indirect reference or relationship to what one has seen" (14.vii.87).

After 30 years of working almost entirely in three dimensions, Bornstein returns, with some trepidation, to painting in watercolours. It is a medium he had barely touched since visiting Maine in 1956. This was when he had painted *The Island*, the culmination—along with the *Tree of Knowledge* for the Saskatchewan Teachers' Federation Building, Saskatoon—of his representational work, so to speak, both completed a year before he constructed his first abstract relief.

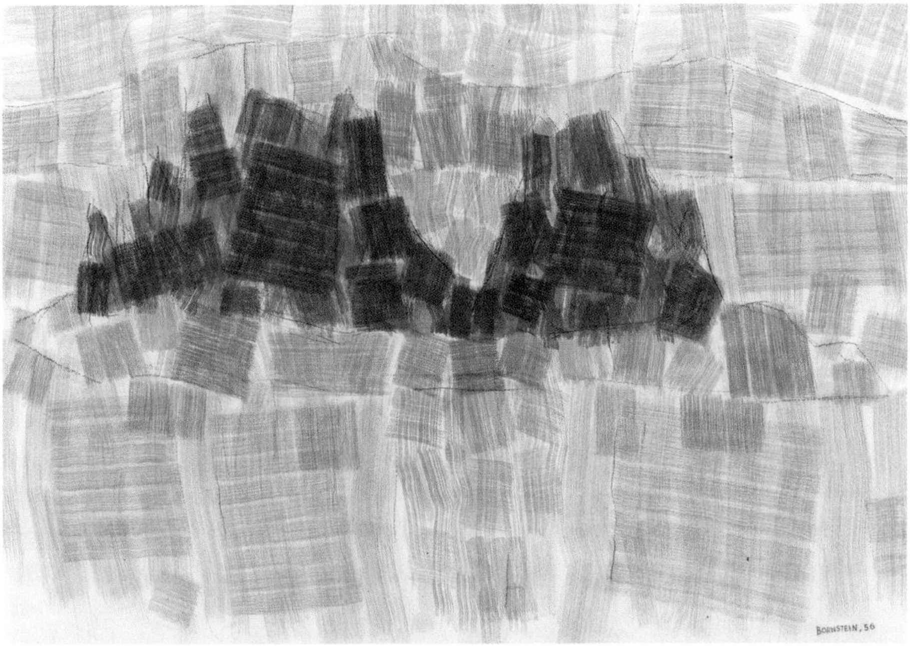

The Island | 1956 WATERCOLOUR ON PAPER, 53.5 × 74 CM

The Island sits on the very cusp of the balance between representation and abstraction. It looks at its subject shrouded in mist, but is constructed with self-sufficient striated brushstrokes, similarly sized and semi-transparent and distributed with compositional regularity across a white ground, Bornstein's delicately poised formal distillation of lessons learned from Cézanne and early Modernism.

Some of his first attempts on Ellesmere may have been "faltering," as he notes, some compromised by wind and rain, but they also learn to capture something of the sensation of things at hand. In the earliest Arctic watercolours to emerge from that summer his technique has not fundamentally changed since 1956. His swatches of colour are similarly striated and loosely rectangular. They are quick and spontaneous and overlap helter-skelter. Imagine them evoking a patch of Arctic ground cover as he encountered them on the first day at Otto Fjord in July 1986, spotted among larger stretches of gravel: "Flowers of rich purples

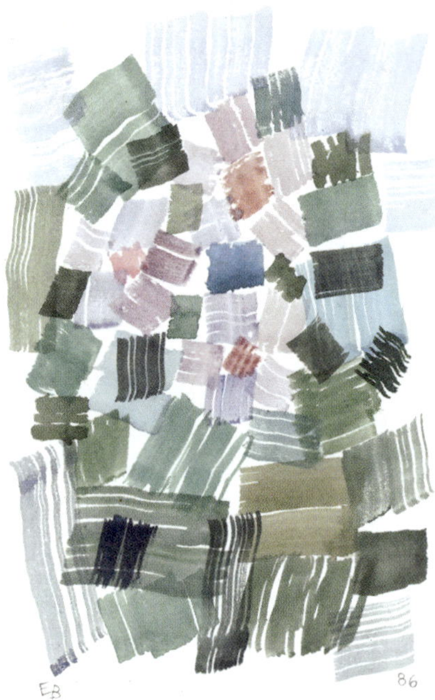

Arctic Study No. 10 | 1986 WATERCOLOUR ON PAPER, 17.4 × 12 CM PRIVATE COLLECTION

amidst varied rich green growth, some of yellows and brilliant coloured moss and lichen" (25.VII.86).

Other watercolours from the first summer take on grander subjects—the sweeping panoramas, the mountainous terrains, the massive shiftiness of the icebergs, the vast skies—the paint patches rising in elation from low horizon lines. Like in *The Island*, they shimmer with cool light, but the swatches are bigger, they no longer overlap, and they start and stop abruptly as if the consequence of more conceptual considerations. As to his subdued colours, Bornstein notes how the icebergs in the fjord, the glaciers and the snow on the mountains are all "a variety of whites and greys" (25.VII.86).

By 1987 Bornstein is into new territory. The paint swatches are now slab-like, striated but solid, chunky and crisp. They can be like building components, but dispersed flat on the white paper, held in place by mutual attractions or repulsions and indifferent to gravity. They are no less lively for that, with implicit twists, pushes and pulls, their colours luminous, fresh and immediate.

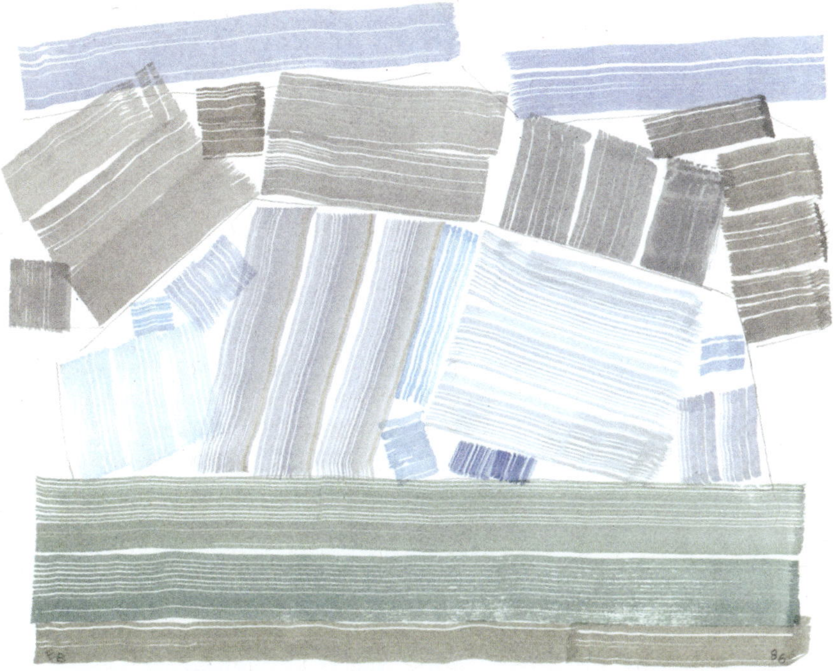

Arctic Study No. 12 | 1986 WATERCOLOUR ON MAT BOARD, 20.6 × 25.4 CM

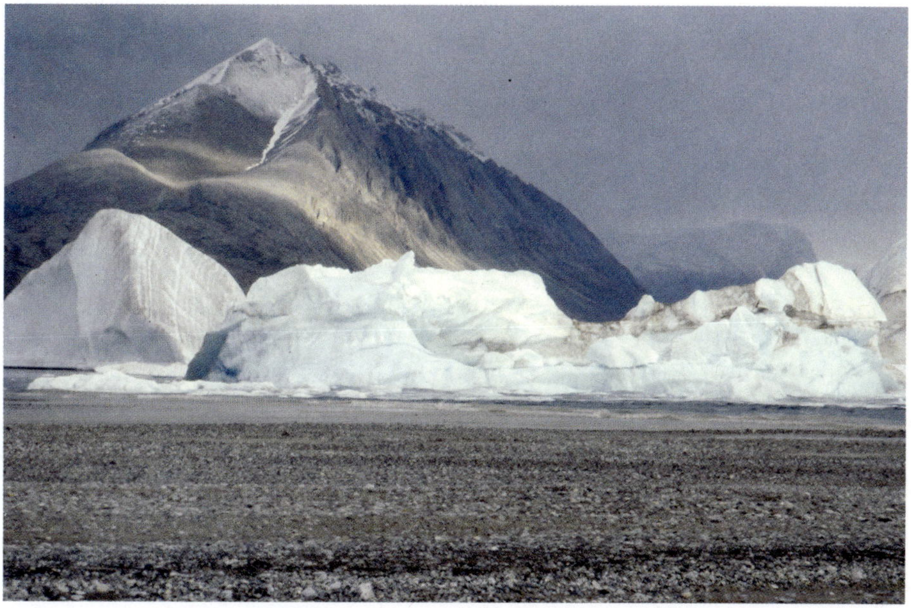

HANS DOMMASCH, **Ellesmere Island** | 1986

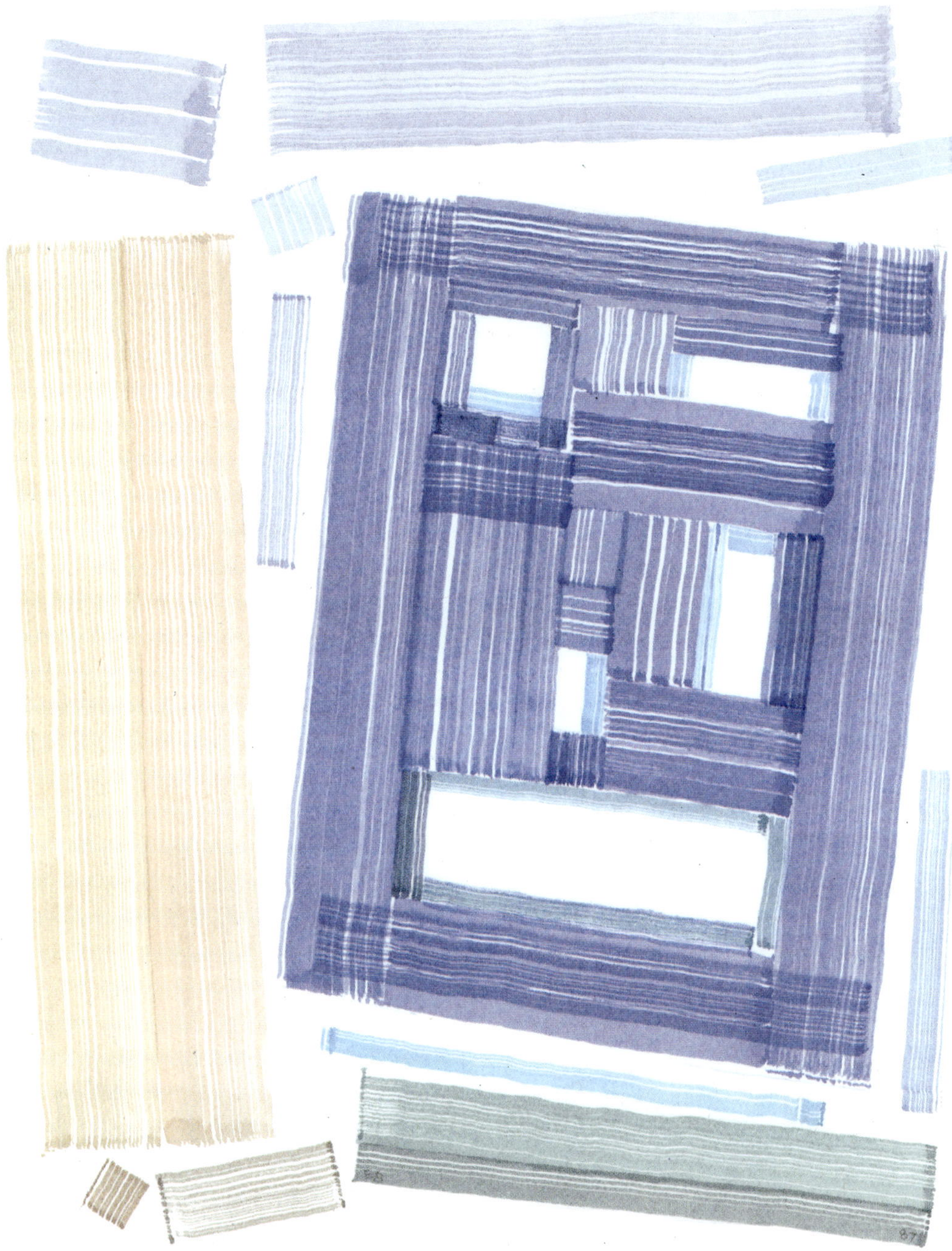

Arctic Study No. 40 | 1987 WATERCOLOUR ON RAG BOARD, 33.6 × 27.3 CM

Sometimes they dance with the lightness of snowflakes. In *Arctic Study No. 40*, the brushstrokes cross to form a cryptic multilayered box configuration, a painted construction adumbrating an actual three-dimensional object. Nature is evoked, not by representation or literal allusion, but by abstractly choreographed analogy. Art, as Julian Barnes said of Cézanne, has "a parallel existence to life rather than an imitative dependence on it."[8]

Or, as Stéphane Mallarmé instructed the artist in front of his subject: "Paint, not the thing, but the effect it produces."[9] While on Alexandra Fjord in 1987, Bornstein reflected at some length on this accord between nature and his art. His subject source, of course, is the thing in front of his eyes. But what he needed to discover was a brushstroke that was "neutral or non-descriptive," which, when used in various sizes, shapes, lengths and directions, would allow him to reconstruct his visions of nature in "a non-literal way." But this is where, as he writes, the use of the descriptor "abstract" as an art-critical category becomes too simplistic: "For me, Arctic space/light/colour/form remain both real and abstract. There is an overwhelming purity of clarity of these elements here that make them at once abstract as well as real. My little studies will appear to many… as abstract. To some others they may even appear as realistic. They are in fact neither or both, which only demonstrates how utterly inadequate, if not useless, such words and modes of perception have become" (14.VII.87).

The on-site studies laid the groundwork for the succession of Arctic-based watercolour paintings executed in Saskatoon. Weather, as Bornstein comments in his journals, is what drives even the most dedicated landscape painters back into their studios, even if it is with regret. "It becomes something different without the direct contact with nature. The Impressionists knew this as did Cézanne. Working in the studio one lacks or misses the physical or sensory stimulus and interaction with nature" (16.VII.87). In 1987 the Arctic work would be exhibited in The Gallery/art placement, Saskatoon: *Eli Bornstein: Arctic Studies. Watercolours 1986–1987*.

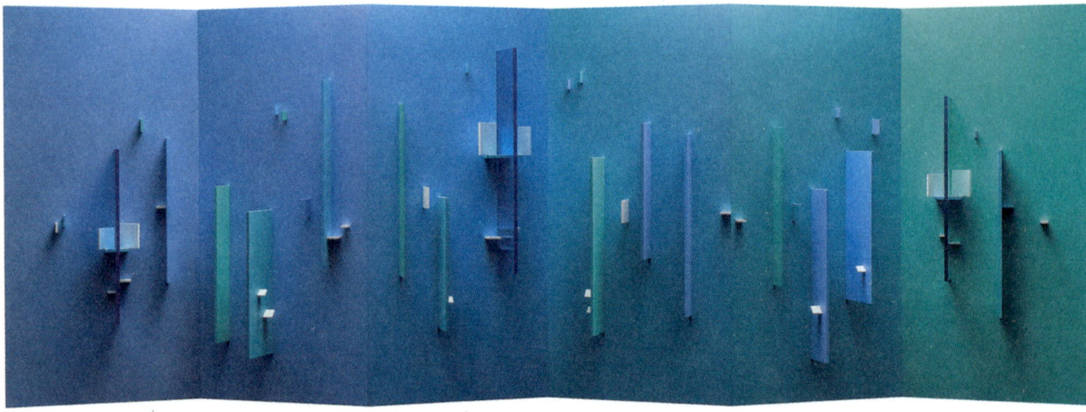

Hexaplane Structurist Relief No. 2 (Arctic Series) | 1995–1998 HOMAGE TO MURRAY ADASKIN. ACRYLIC ENAMEL ON ALUMINUM AND PLEXIGLAS, 67.2 × 182.2 × 15.9 CM UNIVERSITY OF SASKATCHEWAN ART COLLECTION: GIFT OF DOROTHEA ADASKIN | PHOTOGRAPH BY TROY MAMER

BORNSTEIN COMPLETED THE FIRST of his Arctic Series reliefs over the next year: *Multiplane Structurist Relief IV, No. 2 (Arctic Series)*, 1987–1988 (see insert). They were double-plane and multiplane, but what was new to his work was how ingeniously they integrate transparent and coloured Plexiglas into their structures. He had used the material before, but when struck by how, in the clear Arctic air, icebergs could be so sharply mirrored when the water was still, ideas began to percolate about how Plexiglas could serve to evoke comparable effects in the reliefs. Never mind Plexiglas's potential to capture other spectacular ice visions, like how light could glisten off an iceberg "as if its interior were composed of diamonds," or how light on ice could create "lovely blue shadows, haloes and translucent shades" (5.VII.87). In the 1987 issue of *The Structurist* he describes how he was using coloured Plexiglas because of its capacity to colour the space and forms around it, and for how it reflected "the structure in depth, as well as seeming to extend the work beyond its physical limits."[10]

The most magnificent of the Arctic Series is *Hexaplane Structurist Relief No. 2 (Arctic Series)*, 1995–1998, in the collection of the University of Saskatchewan. It is instructive to consider this work within the broader history of Canadian landscape art, or, more particularly, alongside another iconic Arctic picture, Lawren S. Harris's *Icebergs, Davis Strait* from 1930. The exercise is revealing for both.

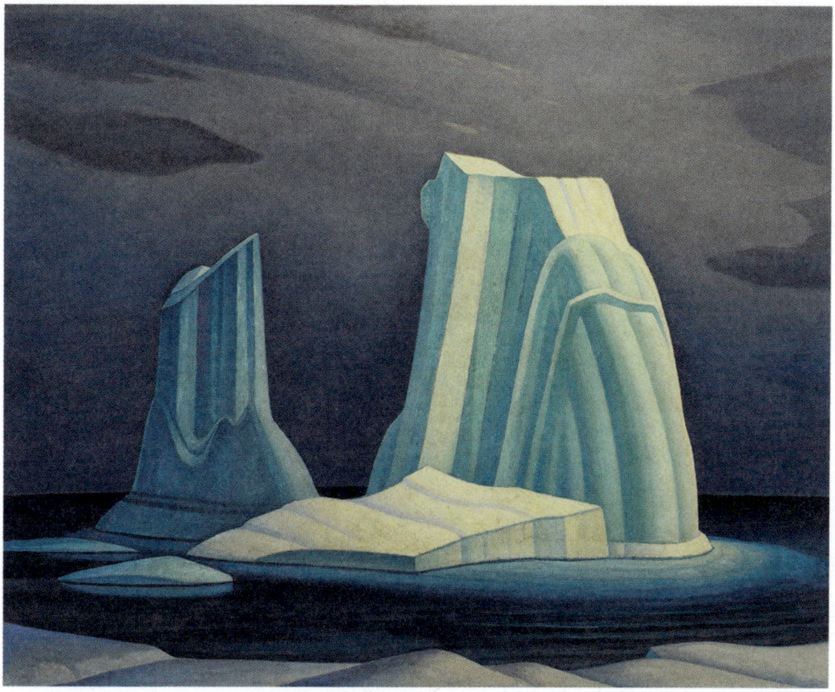

LAWREN S. HARRIS, **Icebergs, Davis Strait** | 1930 OIL ON CANVAS, 121.9 × 152.4 CM

On first flying into Resolute Bay in July 1986, Bornstein described with amazement his sighting of a "solitary majestic iceberg parked in the bay." It stood, as he wrote, "like a sentinel to this primeval land that stretches to the North Pole" (24.VII.86). And later that same morning when, after a few hours of sleep, he set out to explore the land around Resolute Bay—otherwise, as he remarked, "barren" and "rather depressing"—it was once again the iceberg, now seen from ground level, that focused his attention, and offered him his first real awe-inspiring Arctic vision. As he describes the scene in his journal:

> Even though weather here is heavily overcast, there is an aura given off by the ice in the bay that is almost luminescent, and there is something about the long, rounded iceberg that emanates a radiance despite its distance of well over five miles. The iceberg looms on the grey horizon like a giant icon. It is nature's

emissary that speaks eloquently to us of eons of time and space, of vast hemispheric expanses, and of endless processes of formation and movement.

It's exalted language, which rises from naturalistic description into incantation, a kind of "inner seeing," as Lawren Harris might have said. Certainly the Arctic paintings by both Harris and A.Y. Jackson from their Arctic travels in the summer of 1930 were somewhere on Bornstein's mind as he set out to make his own watercolours on Ellesmere Island. Only a few days after his arrival a journal entry (27.VII.86), for all intents and purposes, throws down the gauntlet to his Group of Seven predecessors:

> Thinking of Canadian painters who painted the Arctic and icebergs; in particular, A.Y. Jackson and Lawren Harris come to mind. Especially Harris who loved the icebergs. Why do those paintings seem so empty and to have missed the mark? They seem here to have trivialized the subject. Whereas his ideas, his intent, seemed profound, the works lent themselves too easily to popular cliché.

Bornstein is a little cavalier here, convinced that reconstructing the Arctic landscape in accordance with his own Structurist principles could more authentically embody northern nature than could his predecessors' methods, which were, after all, still essentially representational. Harris was a keen observer of the colours and forms of the icescape he painted, but finally his objective was to transcend mere appearances, marshalling Art Deco stylizations to distill nature into an archetypal icon. Here reside the fundamental differences between the two artists. When Harris stands back, seer-like, in awe of nature's eternities, Bornstein moves up close, like a naturalist, to root his work in an intimate study of nature's ever-changing processes.

But even as the two artists interpreted the Arctic in stylistically different ways, they saw their icy landscapes with shared eyes. The cold palette of Harris's *Icebergs, Davis Strait* registers the same iridescence, the same brittleness, the same limpidity, the same silence, that characterize Bornstein's Structurist reliefs, with their Plexiglas components. There is kinship here, a spiritual resonance between the two artists that serves as a reminder that despite Bornstein's unwavering Modernist abstraction, he, like Harris, is part of another tradition that elsewhere I have called Northern Symbolist Landscape Painting: its unmediated spiritual engagement with wild nature that since the turn of the 19th century has included the unpeopled landscapes of a host of Scandinavians, as well as Ferdinand Hodler and the early Mondrian. In North America it was perpetuated by artists such as Marsden Hartley, Georgia O'Keeffe, Harris and Emily Carr, and was continued, for example, by Charles Gagnon's rococo-glorious skyscapes from the 1970s and 1980s and, in the 21st century, by the digitally constructed sublimities of Christian Eckart.

THE EXPERIENCE OF TRANSCENDENCE, of ascending beyond one's quotidian self, is a theme to which Bornstein regularly returns: his trembling before the awesomeness of the space on Ellesmere Island, his human puniness seen against the icebergs or the mountains (26.VII.86). It recurs in the "profound Arctic shock" he feels in the presence of the fossil forest on Axel Heiberg Island when confronted by the vast distance between human time and geological time. And it is ever-present when enveloped in the North's "unbelievably profound silence," its tranquility like the "'peace that passeth all understanding'" (25.VII.86), a peace which in its original biblical source was "the peace of God" (Philippians 4:7). What reverberates throughout the journals is Bornstein's long immersion in the American subjectivist tradition of Transcendentalism, in the writings of Ralph Waldo Emerson, Henry David Thoreau and Walt Whitman. (He refers at least three times to Thoreau's Walden Pond.) As Emerson writes in his seminal essay "Nature": "In the presence of nature a wild delight runs through the man, in spite of real sorrows."[11] For Bornstein, in the vast Arctic landscape one is "made to forget one's self; one's self-centredness and self-pity vanishes" (8.VII.87). Nature, immediate and underfoot and all around you, as Emerson describes it, "always wears the colours of the spirit."

To artists then, Emerson advises, "go out into the woods alone" and leave behind the trammels of society, for there artists would "become an integral part of God." Bornstein in turn tells us how the "great virgin spaces, stillness, magic light and spectacular beauty" filter out "all the mundane and meaningless activities of one's daily living... and brings one into direct contact with an essential larger reality." Art, in whatever its form, thereby "becomes an act of worship or prayer in recognition of this immense process of which one is such a very momentary part" (8.VII.87).

In his two summers in the Arctic Bornstein met an international host of scientists—geologists, paleontologists, oceanographers, climatologists—as well as film crews, pilots and government officials. These encounters could be compelling, and Bornstein remembers with pleasure his talks with the American writer Barry Lopez (whose book *Arctic Dreams* Bornstein had in his luggage) when the latter spent a night at Alexandra Fjord waiting for his next flight. But most often he resents the intrusions—of which there had been "far too many"—on his isolation and on his one-on-one communion with nature (20.VII.87).

Bornstein's art is spiritually rooted in an unmediated relationship between the individual and nature and thus precludes narrative and social commentary. These are responsibilities that he tackles in his writings, in his essays in the periodical *The Structurist*, and in the journals where he often reflects, with lament, on the future of the North and the Indigenous people who live there. If it is not already too late, as he summarizes the issues in an entry from the third of August 1986,

> will we have the wisdom to protect this land and the wildlife in it, or will we allow it to be exploited by tourism, hunting and fishing, commercial and industrial development and all that follows? When one sees the Inuit... and the deterioration of their way of life, ... their separation from nature, and the many other visible inroads of modern culture, one cannot be hopeful that the Arctic will remain indefinitely wild and unspoiled.

In the mid-1980s, however, the Arctic could still be engaged as Transcendental wilderness, and to return south was to descend from "God's country," bringing back, as an enduring resource for his art, his memories of what had been "a very sacred experience" (3.VIII.86; 1.VIII.86).

ON JANUARY 1, 1990, Bornstein resumed journal writing. As he noted in his very first entry: while he should resolve to write something every day, inevitably other duties and obligations would get in the way. Nevertheless by the end of 2017 his accumulated entries had run to over 1,100 engrossing typewritten pages. Their thoughtful ruminations embraced a plethora of subjects ranging from art and music, to literature and philosophy, to ecology and the human despoliation of the natural world, to travel and personal reminiscences, and to reflections on spiritual transcendency. Throughout the journals the thematic thrust of Bornstein's writing, as of his art, is driven by the power and wonder of natural phenomena as he had most primally experienced them in the Canadian North.

This book concludes with 20 poems that Bornstein composed between 2001 and 2016, drawn from the pages of his journals. They are preceded by a short essay from 2005 in which Bornstein reminisces on his early attraction to poetry and reflects on how the latter's techniques parallel the processes of constructing abstract art.

The reigning image of the poems envisions the sandhill cranes and the great blue herons as they alight on the shores and the sandbars of Bornstein's south Saskatchewan prairie riverbank, and then reascend on their annual migratory routes to and from the Arctic. We might title the poems "musings along the riverbank," their recurring metaphor of migration the launching pad for meditations on the grand themes of human existence. He ends by reflecting on his own mortality. The poems are illustrated with watercolours from Bornstein's Riverbank Series, first exhibited in The Gallery/art placement in Saskatoon in 1990.

Arctic Study No. 14 | 1986 WATERCOLOUR ON RAG BOARD, 25 × 30.4 CM

ARCTIC JOURNALS

PART I | 1986

23.VII.86

WEDNESDAY

STRONG COMPULSION TO make trip to Ellesmere. Not sure why, exactly, but strong feeling of it being very important. As if it is to be a turning point in my life where thereafter all things will be reckoned as B.E. or A.E.—Before Ellesmere or After!

Left Saskatoon 3:15 PM. Short flight to Edmonton. Long stopover in an uninspired air terminal where a three-and-a-half-hour wait is neither particularly pleasant nor comfortable. Would love to have had a sleep (after a restless and sleepless night) but no place to stretch out or lie down. It seems the last thing architects think about in designing air terminals is the comfort or well-being of the traveller.

Had dinner in airport restaurant: meal fair.

Boarded 737 for Yellowknife and Resolute. Plane uses front half for cargo, back end for passengers.

Cloud formations quite spectacular over Edmonton vicinity. Promise and anticipation of things to come?

Land at Yellowknife at 9:30 PM. Surprised at size of place situated at north end of Great Slave Lake and surrounded by tundra. Airport inhospitable. Restaurant closed! An hour later we fly over tundra with rosy sunlit rock and scrubby trees amidst blue-mirrored little lakes scattered endlessly to the horizon and beyond. The sky is lovely blues, mauves and greys. The clouds appear seductively soft and gentle, touched by the circling sun, low in the western sky. How incredible this tireless light, this unending illumination that softens a seemingly harsh landscape.

24.VII.86

THURSDAY

ARRIVE AT RESOLUTE BAY at 1:45 AM. Flying in we see solitary majestic iceberg parked in the bay as if to welcome us. Later learn that someone here took a sample of ice and it is estimated to be 20,000 years old. Ancient monument, older than civilization, stands like a sentinel to this primeval land that stretches to the North Pole. Also learn that sizable chunk of the berg was removed and sent to the Northwest Territories Pavilion at Expo '86 in Vancouver to be used for ice cubes!

We learn that we may not be able to leave for Eureka for a day or so. Excellent food. Hans [Dommasch] and I share a room that is clean and warm. Couldn't sleep. Hans dropped off as soon as lights out at about 2:30 AM, and proceeded to snore uninterruptedly until 9 AM. I tried cotton batting and earplugs, but to no avail. Hope I can find some way to cope with this. Hans is otherwise a most thoughtful and agreeable companion. Perhaps eventually sheer exhaustion will overtake me.

Even though weather here is heavily overcast, there is an aura given off by the ice in the bay that is almost luminescent, and there is something about the long, rounded iceberg that emanates a radiance despite its distance of well over five miles. The iceberg looms on the grey horizon like a giant icon. It is nature's emissary that speaks eloquently to us of eons of time and space, of vast hemispheric expanses, and of endless processes of formation and movement.

Hiked to Resolute Bay, an Inuit community of around 200, about five miles from Resolute air terminal. This part of Cornwallis Island is barren. No discernible vegetation. Rocks and low mountains. Like Rankin Inlet, which I visited in 1964, the place is rather depressing. Relatively new and better housing, but garbage and refuse strewn all over and houses in disrepair. Drying polar bear skins and seal skins seen stretched or hanging over clotheslines in yards. Occasional dogs tied up in yards, scrawny and howling. Generally, a people hopelessly dislocated by the modern world. Our Arctic!

Even though we were five miles closer to iceberg than in the bay, surprisingly it looked smaller and farther away.

25.VII.86

FRIDAY

SLEPT IN SEPARATE ROOMS last night. After good sleep awakened at 7 AM. Very hearty breakfast. Weather: snowing and heavy overcast. Barry [Hough], the base manager and chief dispatcher, informs us we will leave this morning via De Havilland Twin Otter. Met pilot in manager's office, given map and some instructions for reporting weather. (Yesterday we were instructed re: tents, radio operation, rifle, etc.; I am sure not to remember it all, but I have great faith in Hans!) We are to go directly to Otto Fjord on Ellesmere via the Twin Otter rather than go via Eureka since helicopters are not available and in heavy demand elsewhere. Pilot has landed there before. Flight will be about three to three and a half hours. Last minute, pilot changed, and we take off at 9:30 AM.

In all the excitement of boarding, loading gear and preparing for takeoff, I ask myself, "Why did I ever leave the comfort of my home? To get closer to God?"

Doug, the pilot, informs us that there is ice on the elevator [a part of the Twin Otter's tail] and we will have to descend to lower attitude to try to thaw it out so it can be unstuck and usable again. We have left the heavy cloud and the sun is shining.

Dropped to about 200 feet above water that is frozen solid with lovely cerulean blue patches. Elevator okay again, so we go up to clouds, travelling about 150 miles per hour.

Arrive at Otto Fjord at about noon. Doug puts us down beautifully on north shore of fjord that is quite flat and there is a kind of clear landing strip. Unload plane and first order of business is to put up antenna for radio and call Barry at Resolute. Pilot and co-pilot stay until contact established and reception confirmed.

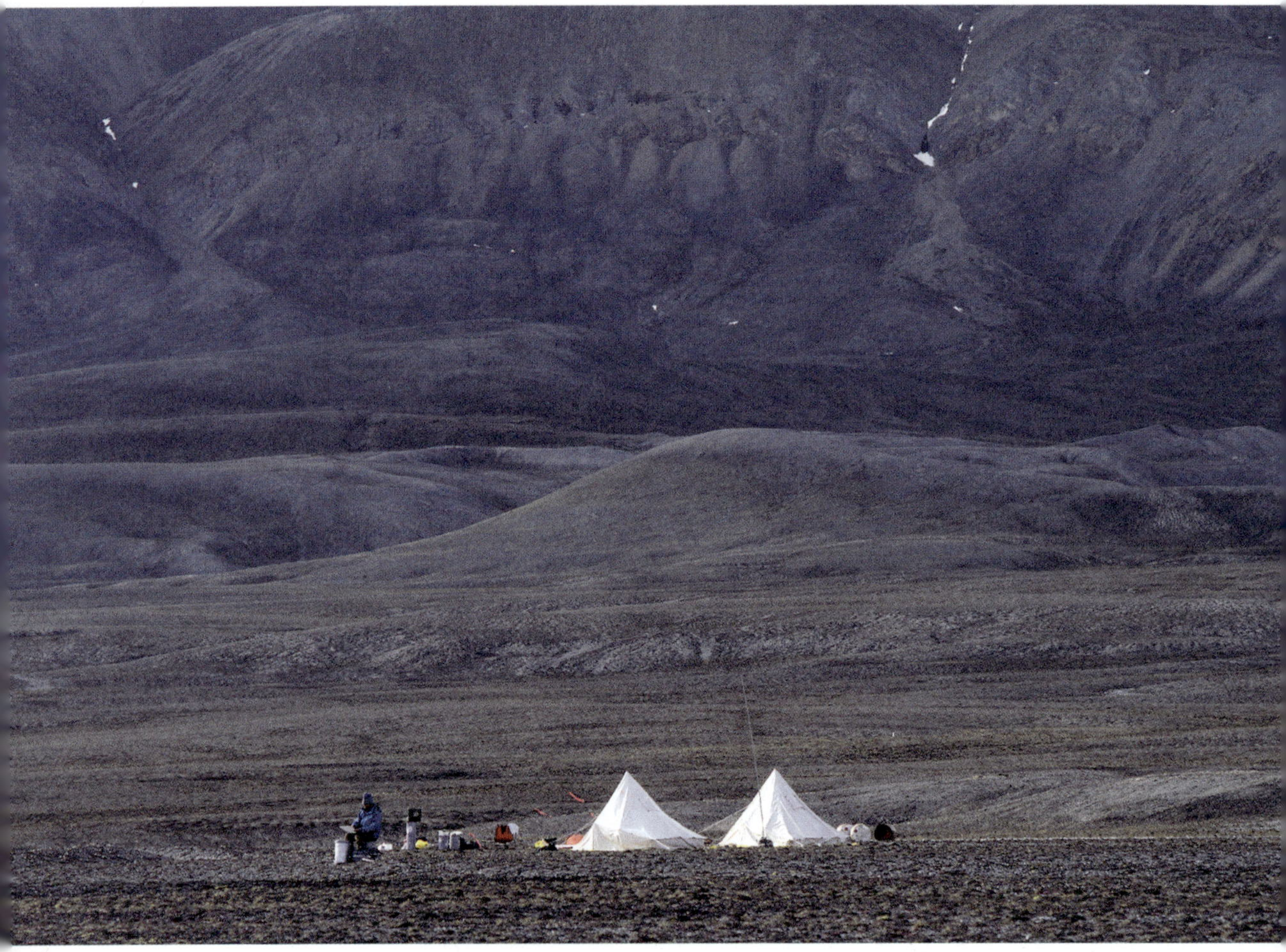

HANS DOMMASCH, **Camp, Otto Fjord** | 1986

Plane takes off nicely in surprisingly short distance and disappears behind mountains on its way back to Resolute via Eureka. Rest of day taken up just putting up two tents, finding water, unpacking groceries, getting stove operational and getting ourselves established.

When we landed it was bright and sunny for first time with temperature around 10 degrees Celsius. This soon changed, and it became overcast again with temperature dropping to 4 degrees and below with wind. Although temperature not that low, it is quite damp and penetrating. I gradually put on all the clothes I brought and remained cold—colder than I feel at home when it drops to 20 or 30 degrees below zero!

Space and distance very misleading here. What seems near turns out to be two or three miles away. Mountains behind us gradually rise to impressive heights with a glacier tongue reaching down between two ranges. Fjord in front of us at least half a mile away. Fjord filled with many icebergs; they are all locked in ice and there is very little open water along shore of fjord. Size of icebergs not as spectacular as one seen in Resolute Bay and somehow disappointing. If they are not free now at the end of July, when will they be again? Hard to guess when they broke off Otto Glacier at the end of the fjord. Those icebergs may have been sitting here for years or decades.

Just as impressive as the mountains, glaciers and icebergs are the tiny Arctic flowers, moss, lichens and most delicate flora spotted generously along the wide rocky gravel stretches between fjord and mountains. Flowers of rich purples amidst varied rich green growth, some of yellows and brilliant coloured moss and lichen. Here the exotic, intricate, miniature coexists with the majestic, the monumental. Their bright and delicate colours are a marked contrast to the dark, brooding mountains rising around us. The ice and bergs of the fjord and the snow on the mountaintops and the glaciers a variety of whites and greys.

In addition to the awesome space, there is the unbelievably profound silence of this place. This silence, this tranquility is like the "peace that passeth all understanding." Very little sign of wildlife. We saw two or three long seagulls and I killed three or four surprisingly large mosquitoes! Can't understand what they live off here.

To bed at 11:30 PM. It is as light as ever. With overcast sky, have yet to follow the complete path of the sun.

26.VII.86

SATURDAY

UP AT 6:45 AM to make our regular radio contact at 7 AM (two required daily—7 AM and 7 PM. XMH 26 is our call number). Quite cool (5 degrees Celsius) and overcast.

Yesterday afternoon Hans took many photos. Today he started taking photos of icebergs west of our camp and while doing so saw a grey seal who emerged near shore in the open water. This means there must be fish in the fjord.

Hiked to east end or source of fjord and saw three Arctic terns (or curlews), also a duck. At head of fjord is the glacier and there are more icebergs here with more open water surrounding them. Clouds breaking and sun and blue sky appearing in southern sky. Temperature going up to 18 degrees Celsius. For the first time in two days I am actually warm and removed my jacket and cap. Reflections of icebergs in water magnificent. These images remind me of my double-plane reliefs, particularly those explorations involving mirror or reflected images. These towering icebergs reflected in the water where the reflection is even clearer than the actual berg suggest many new possibilities for reliefs, using white Plexiglas, possibly transparent and translucent colour Plexiglas and painted colour parts. If only they could be realized as quickly here on the spot as watercolours, or better yet, as photographs. In that sense, making reliefs is a primitive art requiring hundreds and even thousands of hours to realize one work. Walk about two or three miles back to camp.

We plan to pack a lunch tomorrow morning and hike to this spot to spend all day there—Hans photographing, me painting.

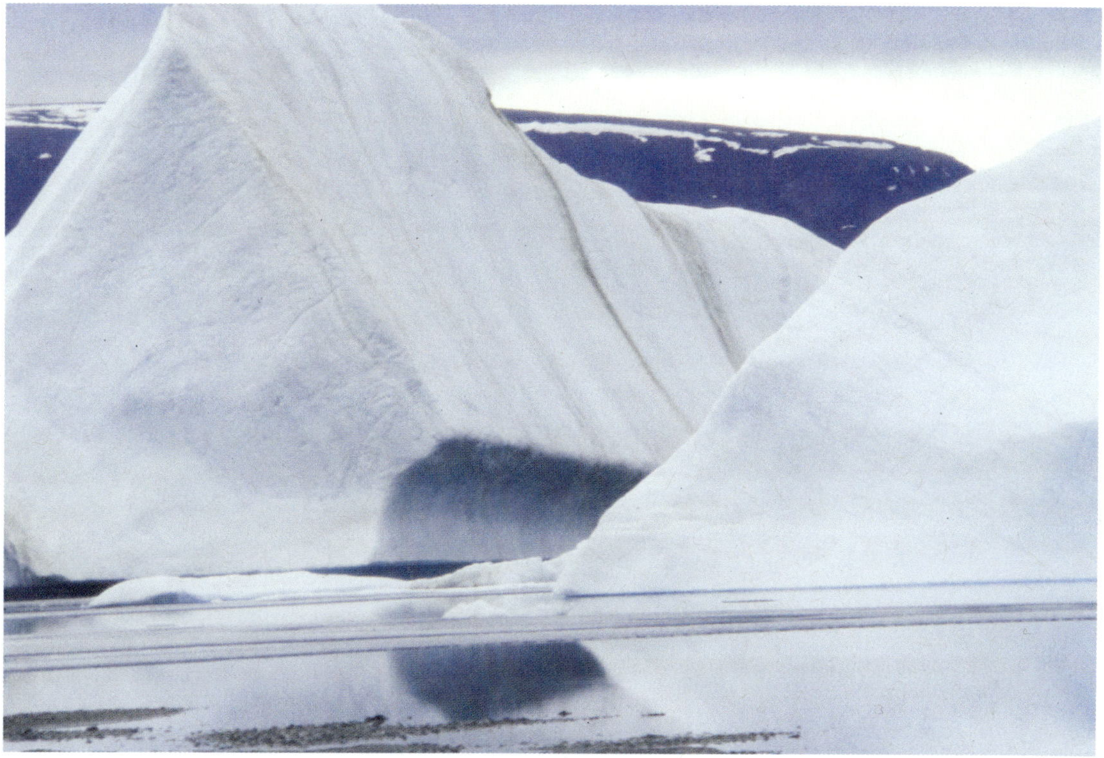

HANS DOMMASCH, **Icebergs, Ellesmere Island** | 1986

This afternoon as Hans went off to photograph flowers, I unpacked and sorted out my painting things. Forgot to bring numerous things. Should have brought jar for water, backpack and folding stool. Arrange to take smaller paper and sufficient paint and brushes to fit into my little blue bag and am off to look and paint my first watercolour.

Have many paintings in my head—beautiful! Actually painting is another matter. Must make many more before I can even approach what's in my head. I want to do studies for or toward reliefs based on icebergs and what I see here but not literal descriptions. Hans is doing that marvellously.

We meet at camp around 5:30 PM and have a drink, relax and prepare for dinner so we are finished by 7 PM and our radio call—what Barry calls the "skid"

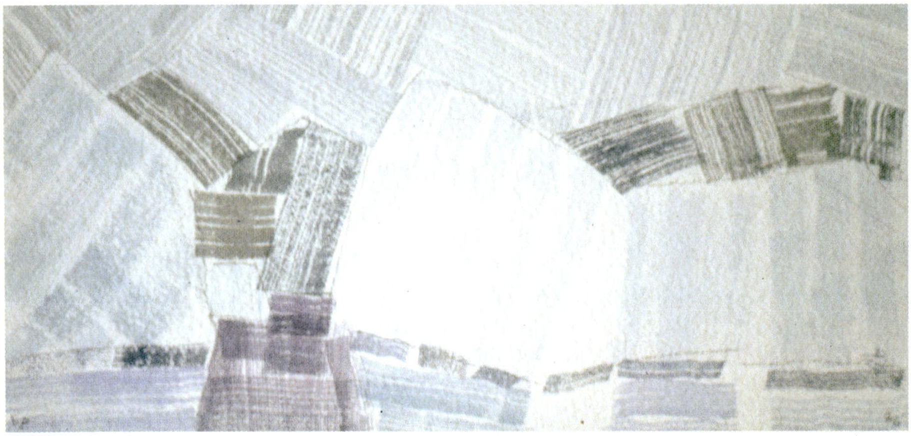

Arctic Study No. 4 | 1986 WATERCOLOUR ON PAPER, 13.3 × 27.9 CM

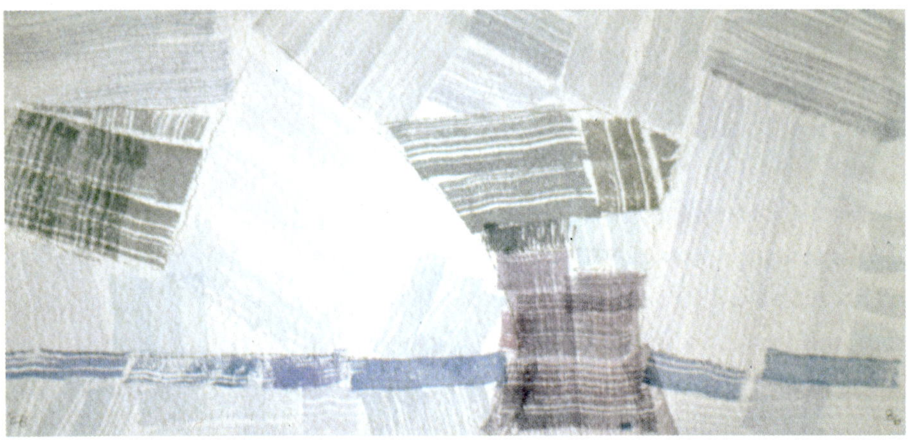

Arctic Study No. 5 | 1986 WATERCOLOUR ON PAPER, 13.3 × 27.3 CM

when he calls each of the camps scattered across the Arctic. When I asked him how he was this evening he said he was "fighting alligators" in Resolute. He has a tough job requiring 17-hour days, babysitting all the groups and coordinating air travel, fuel, etc. No wonder he has developed such a grim sense of humour.

The light here is a unique phenomenon to behold with the sun never setting, but arching the sky from east to west in the southern sky in the morning, and from west to east in the northern sky in the evening. This means icebergs and mountain can be illuminated from all sides during the 24-hour cycle. It is unbelievable as one sees the bergs illuminated constantly and differently without the break of night or darkness. What would Monet have made of these ice-stacks and mountain-cathedrals?

How puny is man when seen against the icebergs or the mountains and how insignificant he appears in this vast Arctic landscape. And yet in man's mind and spirit, there is something of a parallel vastness, is there not?

27.VII.86
SUNDAY

AFTER A RESTLESS NIGHT, having to leave my warm sleeping bag to pee two or three times, awakened just before 7 AM in time for the morning skid. Barry informs us that he can't move us to the east coast until the 30th and suggests we consider staying another week. We will "traffic" (radio lingo for talking business) about it tonight. Hans and I consider the matter and decide it would be too complicated to try to change reservations for flight and hotel, etc., as well as postponing other commitments. If Barry is willing to get us to Alexandra Fjord for two days and get us back to Resolute by August 2nd, that will be fine. If not, we will continue our exploration of Otto Fjord.

After breakfast, did another watercolour of "our" iceberg, the majestic one nearest by, which I did yesterday. 10:30 AM return to camp to pack a sandwich and off to meet Hans, near head of Otto Fjord where there is some open water and many icebergs—about four miles from camp. Light is different today even though sunny. Reflections in water are not as good. Start another watercolour about 11:30 AM while Hans makes his way toward glacier. Work for about an hour and it starts to rain. Suddenly notice for the first time that these icebergs are moving and berg I am painting has turned 45 degrees while others I saw yesterday are in different places and positions! It is astounding that these enormous mountains of ice are that mobile in this fjord where there is no ocean current, and yet farther down the fjord the icebergs are locked in ice or grounded.

Pack up my unfinished sketch and materials. Eat my lunch in rain and meet up with Hans and make our way back to camp. After tea, we decide to hike to glacier north of camp. It has no name so we call it Little Otto. We leave at 3 PM and although it looks not too far away, it turns out to be about five miles with many hidden valleys before we get within sight of the incredible tongue of the glacier. The primordial power of water, snow, ice, rain and the invincible glacier that moves earth and mountains reveals its awesome force wherever we look.

We return to the two barely visible white triangles in the distance—our tents—which are lost in the vast expanse stretching below.

Barry informs us he will pick us up Thursday at 9 PM and take us via Eureka and several other stops to the east coast and Alexandra Fjord. We will only have about 24 hours there before being picked up to return to Resolute.

Thinking of Canadian painters who painted the Arctic and icebergs; in particular, A.Y. Jackson and Lawren Harris come to mind. Especially Harris who loved the icebergs. Why do those paintings seem so empty and to have missed the mark? They seem here to have trivialized the subject. Whereas his ideas, his intent, seemed profound, the work lent itself too easily to popular cliché. They never approached the intensity or depth, the resonance, of Monet's haystacks or Cézanne's Mont Sainte-Victoire.

Photography has made images of the remote and inaccessible easily available. Calendar pictures and postcards of faraway places are commonplace. Art must have another role or function. The artist in the actual presence of wild and unspoiled nature must find new means or media to express something of the natural wonder. All the old ways have been exhausted. Easy to say! New vision and creation is not easily born and may take decades, if not centuries to appear. Here in the Arctic, one is aware that centuries are like seconds in the geological time frame that surrounds one. No hurry here!

28.VII.86

MONDAY

LAST NIGHT THE TEMPERATURE dropped to 4 degrees Celsius. I got so cold around 9:30 PM that I was shaking and my teeth chattering even though I was wearing all the clothes I brought. The only warm place is inside my sleeping bag. Slept better last night.

This morning cold (4 degrees Celsius) and overcast. After breakfast we hiked back to where we were yesterday morning. Everything was different. The stream from the other glacier feeding into the fjord has risen, the icebergs were all in different places. It was as if some great hand had simply moved the monolithic bergs like pawns in a chess game or like parts of a great harmonious construction. And again the light was totally different. The transformation in 24 hours was of such a scale as to overwhelm one utterly.

Painted three watercolours crouched on the large delta of the stream until I was overcome by the damp cold and began shivering. Interrupted painting to eat the sandwich I brought and move around to try to warm myself. Water in the many streams flowing into the wide delta opening into the fjord echoes in the space surrounded by mountains. Sun emerges and temperature gradually rises to 10 degrees Celsius. Finish watercolours and return to camp, in time for tea with Hans.

Since we will be leaving tomorrow afternoon, there is an urgency we both feel about seeing and doing as much as we can here. We have both come to love this place and fallen completely under its unimaginable splendour—its magic of light, colour, space of a scope beyond full human comprehension. We are indeed on top of the world!

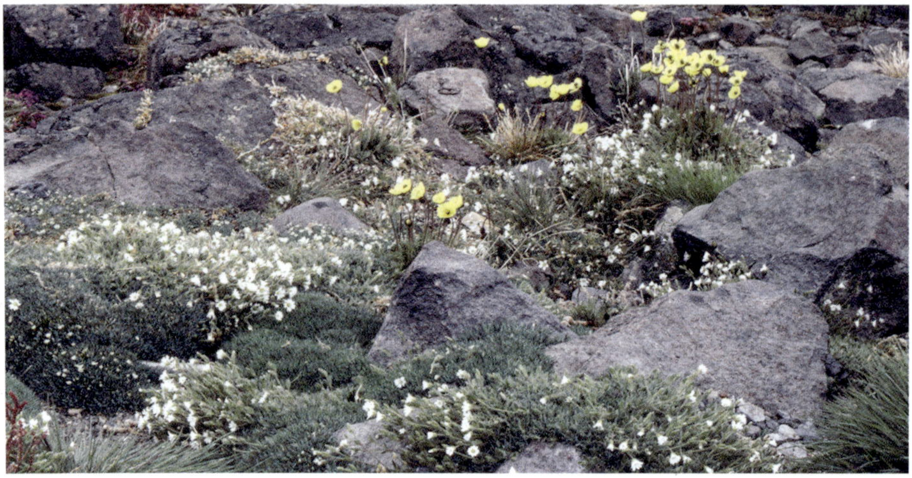

HANS DOMMASCH, **Late July Flora** | 1986

Today I discover that the beautiful little Arctic flowers (saxifrage) of different purples that I admired the day we arrived must have reached their fullest bloom on that day, for they are now shrivelled and wilted. What a welcome we received and didn't know it.

Hans went off to shoot more icebergs and mountains, while I stayed close to camp to do two more watercolours, which seemed to go best of all so far. It was about 30 years ago that I did my last serious painting in watercolour in Maine, summer of 1956. Getting back to it after all that has intervened with my concentration on constructed reliefs is curious, sometimes frightening, sometimes surprising and delightful. Resonances of the past mingling with new currents of awareness. Looking at these faltering attempts after getting back home will reveal more clearly what, if anything, has been achieved and should be nurtured as a complementary, reinforcing activity.

Hans returns at 7 PM exhausted but euphoric over the shots he has managed to take.

Weather keeps shifting, from sunshine to clouds or rain or snow, to fog and mists transforming this fjord into an ever-changing panorama—all different yet spectacular and spellbinding—revealing new things never seen before.

The circling sun touching now this facet of iceberg or mountain, now that, in a never-ending sequence of changing light direction, quality or quantity. Surely there could be no better place for an artist to learn from nature about the possibilities of art than the Arctic. Here I am at 63 in this ultimate kindergarten!

29.VII.86

TUESDAY

AWAKENED BY SNOW pattering on tent at 2:30 AM. At 7 AM, still snowing, temperature 2 degrees Celsius, solid overcast sky with visibility about one mile. Mountains are obscured in fog. Our closest iceberg, which I call Moby Dick because it has something of the shape and character of an enormous white whale, looms in the mist like some apparition.

It does not look very promising for the plane to land and move us today. Barry requests I call him back at 11 AM to see if things improve. Hate the thought of taking down tents and packing in the wet snow.

Things I miss the most up here:

Christina—how I wish you were here.

Warmth—I seem to be perpetually cold with no source of heat. Nothing to build a fire with. Cooking stove outside throws very little heat.

Dryness—dampness is pervasive, even when it is not raining or snowing.

Chair—no place to sit down, particularly when out painting. Have to kneel or crouch on rocks for hours at a time so that I can hardly straighten up or walk. Would be nice to be able to sit and read or write. We do sit on food cans in desperation. Even a small folding stool would have been a blessing.

Sarah and Thea—although I see little enough of them at home, their presence is missed.

MacTavish—my four-legged pal would love it up here and would be great company. How he would enjoy the 15 to 20 miles of walking every day.

We are each in our own tents waiting for it to stop raining or snowing. I hear Hans snoring. How I envy his gift of dropping off into a deep sleep in minutes. Last night again spent many sleepless hours.

Yesterday, Hans saw the tracks of a muskox on his walk to the head of Otto Glacier. (I could not accompany him because the streams were so high and discovered several days ago that my rubber boots have a leak and got my feet wet several times.) Also, he brought back a piece of fur that looks like it came from a wolf. On our walks there is evidence of some rodent that lives on the tundra burrowing holes. Haven't seen one yet. Although did encounter a few mosquitoes when we first came, have hardly seen any since. Lots of little flies around who seem to like my watercolours. Fortunately, they don't bite, nor seem to be around when we're eating or get into the food. They seem to have only a taste for art!

Barry informed us that there is an emergency on Ice Island so we can't be moved today. Also, he talked to someone in the vicinity of Alexandra Fjord who said there were no icebergs in the locale. We would need a helicopter to try to spot them farther south and no helicopters are free for the next week. So, we have abandoned plans to travel to the east coast to see the larger bergs moving in the ocean currents. It would be too complicated now and involve packing, taking down tents, etc., and putting them up again for only a day or so and there would be the risk of missing our flight home on August 2nd.

So, we are content to continue exploring Otto Fjord and discovering new and fascinating aspects daily. We will endeavour to come back next year and spend all the time on the east coast. We should also be better prepared and have more idea of what to expect. Barry said he would give us names to contact and places to consider for next year, including Greenland.

Snow turned to rain and eventually stopped. Weather improved a bit. After lunch, we went out again to the head of the fjord. I was astounded to see that all the bergs had moved again and were rearranged. It was as if these huge bergs the size of five- or ten-storey buildings were choreographed in this mammoth dance. Some moved half turns, others a quarter, and still others one step back and a complete pirouette!

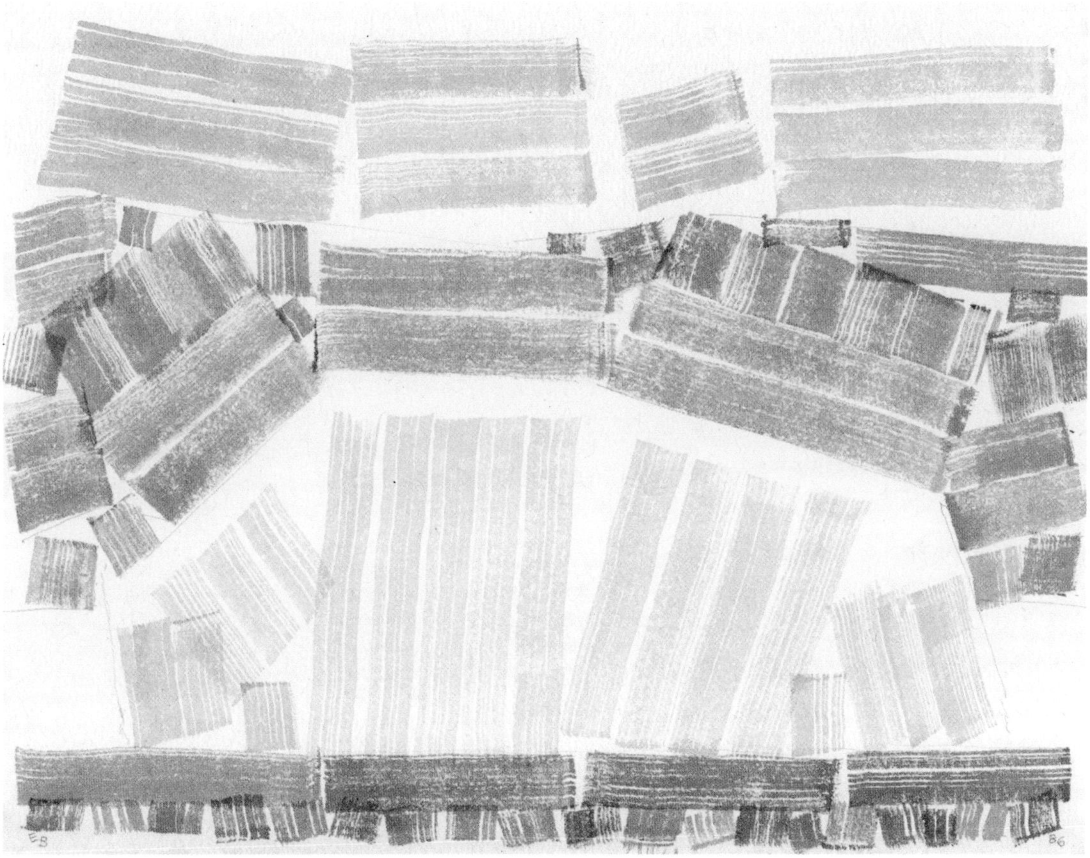

Arctic Study No. 7 | 1986 WATERCOLOUR ON MAT BOARD, 28.5 × 37.78 CM

Surely, this dance of the icebergs is a manifestation of primordial forces of nature, of which we are a part (Shaw called it the "life force"). It is that creative force that we should worship and celebrate in our daily lives by our acts and behaviour. To ascribe to this force a human deity, as most religions do, seems to be a travesty and reveals man's conceit and blindness. Some Indigenous spiritualities seem closer to the reality than our rigid, doctrinaire, sectarian, divisive religions, none of which are large enough to encompass the unspeakable grandeur of nature.

Hans returned to tell me that while photographing there was a tremendous rumbling and one of the bergs turned over on its side and revealed some beautiful varieties of blue ice which evidently have something to do with its age, compression and loss of oxygen. He was so excited by this event he was beside himself and in tears of sheer joy. I was envious and regretted not being there to see the spectacle. In his excitement at witnessing the dramatic upheaval of one of the large icebergs, Hans said: "My God, it's as great as sex!" This reminded me of some thoughts that occurred to me while riding a subway in Toronto some years ago. What we call sex is that unspoiled bit of nature deep within each human being, which often gets thwarted, twisted and blocked by civilization or culture. It often becomes inaccessible or corrupted into various forms of pornography. Whereas it is perhaps the purest expression within us of creation that united us with the wildness of nature. It is like the last vestige of true nature within us that is no less endangered than the destruction or pollution of our environments, our wildlife and our ecological connections. For sex is as natural a force as the wind or rain or movement of the icebergs. Perhaps some music and art, at their best, recall or stir in us some slight sense of ancient nature and, while an expression of culture, actually serve to cut through all the discontents of civilization and provide a window to our deepest selves.

I finished another watercolour and we met back at camp for a drink, the daily skid and later "traffic" on the wireless. Then dinner and the evening chores before bed.

30.VII.86
WEDNESDAY

AFTER THE SKID and breakfast, we packed up our gear and went off to the "meadow" on the slope nearest the head of Otto Fjord. It means crossing the stream that every day gets deeper, wider and faster. Last night I suggested after dinner that we carry a long two-foot by eight-foot board that happened to be abandoned here near the airstrip to the beginning of the wide gravel bed across which we have to travel and use it as a bridge over the stream. Hans agreed so we left it there and came back. This morning we picked it up and carried it to a crossing point and it worked well for me. Hans preferred wading through with his good rubber boots. We left the board behind as it is quite heavy, in addition to the things we are carrying—Hans with his various cameras, lenses, film and tripod; me and my art materials, which I estimate to weigh about 35 pounds. On a ten-mile hike, this gets increasingly heavier.

On the meadow, with the sun shining again, we see muskox tracks and droppings where they must have been grazing on the vegetation. Also, we see rabbit droppings. We part as I make off toward the icebergs for another watercolour. On the way, I encounter two or three different kinds of birds who cry out and circle me as I must be near their nests. They are quite lovely. One, like a swallow but larger. Another, with strong black and white markings. The third about the size of a large robin with rusty orange breast and long black bill.

Work for several hours near a group of pyramid-shaped icebergs beautifully reflected in the water nearby. The sun is out lighting everything beautifully and warming me up. Eventually clouds close in and the temperature drops and all is changed. Have my sandwich and begin the long trek back. If only I can remember where the bridge board was left. Hans is out of sight, probably in one of the valleys miles behind. As luck would have it, I can't find the board and keep going upstream looking for it until I realize I'm miles too far. Decide to make the best of crossing where I am and wading across in my leaky boots. Make it across with wet feet and head in the direction of camp that is so far away it can't be seen.

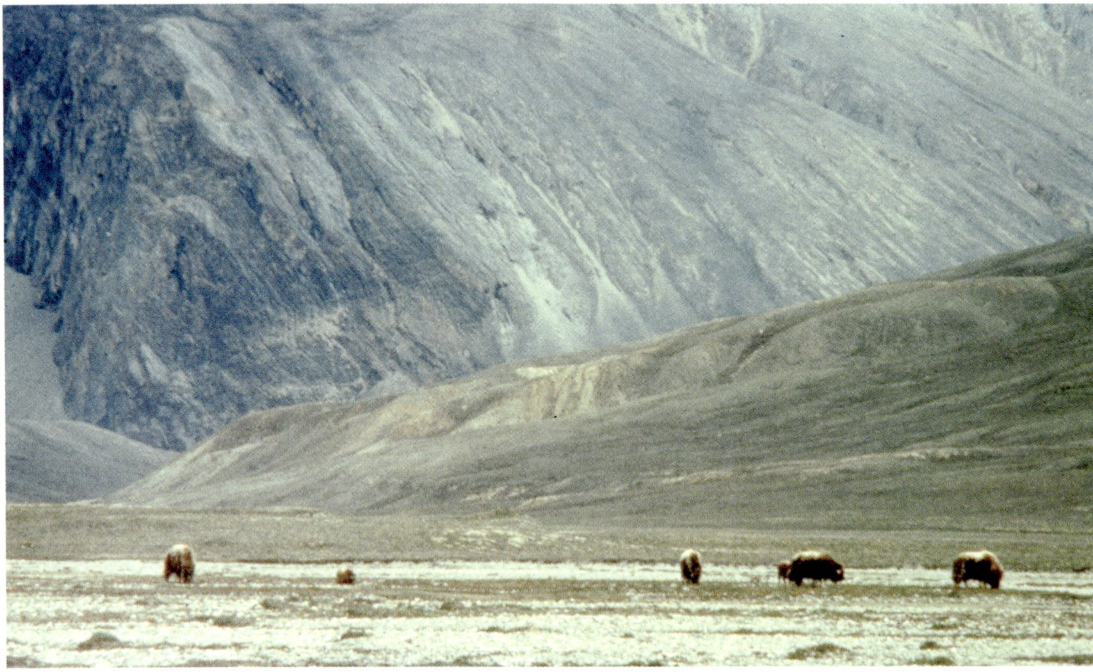

HANS DOMMASCH, **Muskox, Otto Fjord** | 1986

After some time, I spot our two white triangles on the tundra and realize I have gone out of my way considerably and have added several miles to the distance. It is so difficult to judge distance here. Easier to misjudge.

Something about this place and the icebergs often makes me think of Ibsen's *Peer Gynt and Brand*. An obvious association, I suppose. Just as I often think of Melville and his marvellous description of the sea and the great white whale, which I read about 35 years ago!

Had another try at Moby Dick—that stolid, implacable, inscrutable, monumental iceberg that has not moved an inch since we arrived. The circling sun and ever-changing cloud conditions play different light on its broad back giving it the variety of colours of the spectrum.

Where we were today we saw icebergs that were several city blocks long but couldn't get very close to them.

Hans returned from his safari, exhausted but elated. In his wandering he came upon a herd of six muskox feeding on the green slopes. When the bull, accompanied by three adults and two calves, stopped eating and looked up at him, Hans decided it was time to go. He was about 200–300 feet from them and said he got some good shots. Very sorry to miss the encounter with the remarkable survivor of the North American ice ages.

On the skid tonight, confirmed with Barry that we will stay here until Friday and probably return to Resolute that afternoon. Tomorrow is our last day here so we want to absorb and do all we can, weather permitting. Everything hinges upon the weather up here, which is fickle and frivolous in its changes—constantly altering from moment to moment. It is quite typical to have four entirely different skies ranging from rain, snow, or fog, scattered clouds and sunshine simultaneously in the four directions. The weather performs here like a four-ring circus, 24 hours a day. It is the greatest show on top of this earth. I must ask someone knowledgeable in meteorology or geography why it is warmest during the midday and cools off at night even though the sun does not set. Also, why we have never seen the sun and clear sky in the North at night. It has always been overcast. Could it be because we are so close to the North Pole? Wind coming up at 10 PM estimated 15–20 knots from the east. Hope it doesn't blow the tents over!

31.VII.86
THURSDAY

USUAL OVERCAST MORNING; 7 degrees Celsius and slight rain. Slight wind from north, which we haven't had before. Since it keeps drizzling and I can't paint, we decide to hike to the valley of the muskox so that I might yet see the family if they are still there, and one last look at the icebergs at the head of Otto Fjord. I leave my watercolours behind, and Hans only carries his Leica so won't be bogged down with carrying so much gear. The hike takes a total of over four hours or about 16 miles there and back. The great wide valley is lovely but no muskox in sight. They have moved into another valley that would be another two hours away at least. So, we go as far as the summit we call Dommasch Point that has a lovely view of the glacier and the icebergs nearby. The summit is made up of rock chips from the nearby mountain.

The rocks here in the trillions are amazing. There are so many varieties of kinds, size, shape, colour, etc. Good thing Christina is not here or between us with our penchant for rock collecting, the Twin Otter would never get off the ground.

Many of the rocks have marvellous markings of lichen of various colours, graphic shapes and patterns. Also, in the valley we pass through are different kinds of flowers and birds. There is a lovely yellow buttercup that emerges from a furry bud. Also, maybells. Have seen numerous bees.

We see many more muskox tracks and droppings. Also, droppings of wolves and rabbits. On my long trek back to camp, I see muskox tracks going right to the edge of the fjord. Can't understand why he or she would come down to the fjord. Surely not for a drink when there are so many fresh streams near their grazing areas. Could they be like Hans and me, and simply like to look at the icebergs? Or have they developed an exotic taste for water from melted ancient icebergs, whose ice contains compressed oxygen? We were told that the ice from ancient bergs releases the oxygen when placed in water. The ice that was shipped to Expo '86 from Resolute was to be used as ice for drinks at the Northwest Territories Pavilion where they would probably charge around $5 for a cocktail with iceberg ice! Here the ice is free!

On my way back, I encounter a beautiful bird sitting on a clump of green grass singing and nearby is a huge purple flower. The bird has black on top of its head, a white breast and face and grey wings and is the size of a large seagull. It's amazing how the birds and rocks often echo the colours of the mountains, sky and bergs.

After returning to camp cold, wet and tired, I have some hot soup and lunch and revive myself. My back has begun to ache increasingly over the past few days even though I try to do my exercises daily. Curiously enough, my chronic elbow has not ached once while here. After changing wet socks and boots, went off for another try at Moby. Made a few pencil sketches for painting while on the hike this morning but it is so cold that it's unlikely I will get a chance to try to paint them before we leave tomorrow. Imagine hiking 15 miles for a few little sketches. If only it were a little warmer and I would not get so cold sitting or crouching and working.

The circling sun acts curiously here. Even though there is an overcast sky, it will break through like a spotlight and suddenly illuminate one iceberg or part of the glacier or the tip of a side of a mountain, often nowhere near where the sun is. Sometimes this only lasts for a few minutes, but is very dramatic. One never knows what will be spotlighted and be centre stage in this fjord that is about 15–20 miles wide between mountain ranges and visibly extends about ten miles east and west from where we are. Such a theatre and such performances are without end for the summer season.

There are so many things about this place that are so fleeting—here for a short while and gone: the appearance of the animals, the light and cloud conditions, the reflection of icebergs, the appearance of wildflowers, etc. So much depends on being in the right place at the right time or simply good fortune. For the great show goes on here even while one sleeps or one's back is turned, or is in the next valley, and one has missed another act, the exact like of which may never play again.

1.VIII.86
FRIDAY

WE ARE CONFIRMED to be picked up at around 3 PM. Morning is reasonably good weather so after breakfast I return to confront Moby one more time and am painting by 9 AM. Finish one watercolour around 10:30 and decide there is enough time for one last try.

Return to camp at 12:30 PM. Hans has already started to pack. We have lunch and I begin to pack. At 1:30 PM Twin Otter arrives on scene early and after beautiful landing, taxis up to our tent. Young couple, Guenther and Ann,

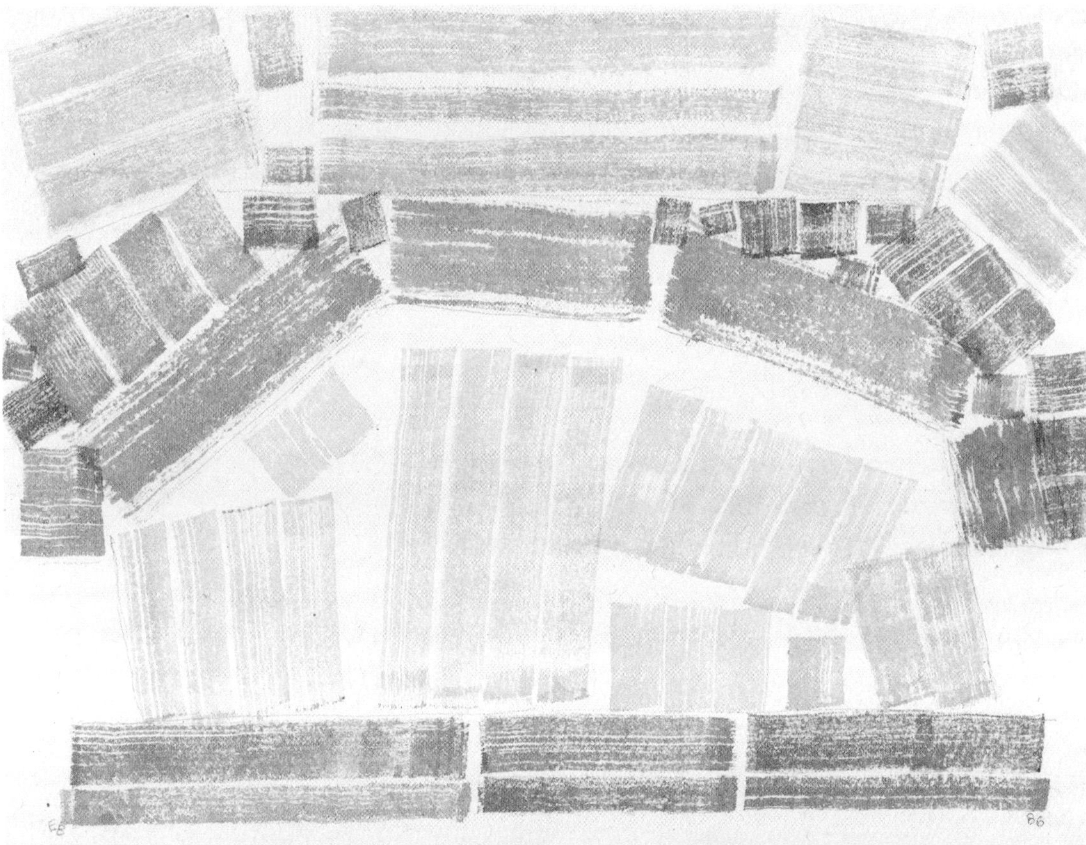

Arctic Study No. 8 | 1986 WATERCOLOUR ON RAG BOARD, 28.5 × 37.4 CM

descend from plane. They are geologists from Dalhousie who were picked up first at Phillips Inlet. Ann is very friendly and being the first person and woman we have seen in eight days, is a lovely sight. She and her husband Guenther pitch in and take down and pack up our tents and radio. The pilot and co-pilot also pitch in and before we know it we are taxiing down the short rocky strip and in the air over the fjord by 2 PM. It is a very emotional experience. Tears in my eyes as we leave this truly incredible place. The flight is rough over the mountains, but the views are breathtaking as we head for Eureka where the geologist couple is to be dropped off and we are to pick up Jim Basinger and his party of six on their way back to Saskatoon via Resolute after six weeks on Axel Heiberg Island. Eureka seems desolate, windswept place with wind gusting at over 30 knots. We land and help couple unload and meet Jim on runway. He is busy packing up cartons of rock samples with plant fossils. We help as the wind howls around us. And then wait for the rest of the party and all their baggage while plane refuels. We have a good visit on plane with Jim, Beth McIver and John Davies sitting together and the other four younger students seated behind us. We exchange and compare experiences. Beth breaks open a lunch given to her by some army geologists. She shares it with all and includes such exotic foods as fried chicken and fresh peaches. We arrive in Resolute at 6:35 PM after going through poor weather and low ceiling. Pilots make a fantastic landing through fog after nearly missing air strip. We are met at plane, assigned our rooms and baggage is driven over to the PCSP [Polar Continental Shelf Project] complex where dinner is waiting for us. And what a fabulous dinner: Arctic char pie, halibut, brussels sprouts, fresh salad, fresh fruit and strawberry cream puffs.

We have interesting conversations. John Davies gives me a rock with fossils of redwood tree needles and a piece of redwood from a tropical forest they explored that is about 45 million years old. The wood has been preserved by the cold—is not fossilized! It could still be carved or burned. I handle it carefully and treasure it like some holy object. There is an aura about it that only time, and great stretches of it, can bestow on things. Similarly, people in very old age often radiate something of such aura.

Meeting and talking to all these different people postpones the realization that our trip, a very sacred experience, is over. When we flew over our fjord it occurred to me that probably all the churches and cathedrals man has ever built to the glory of God would fit onto Otto Fjord, which is only a small part of Ellesmere Island, which is only a portion of the Arctic. This land and its great unspoiled beauty is at times terrifying and at other times, makes you cry. I feel like I have just returned from the greatest church on earth. It is truly a humbling and yet uplifting experience of the spirit. We were privileged to see even a small part of it and hope we can return.

When I re-read the above, I realize how difficult, if not impossible, it is to convey the depth and scope of this experience. Words like "holy," "sacred," "spiritual," "religious" and "God" are words that have lost their power through much overuse and abuse in our profane culture.

I have not looked at any of the watercolours I have painted and wonder how they will look to me. Those who look at them who expect some photographic recording or detailed rendering of the appearances of the landscape here will surely be disappointed and even find my efforts shocking. Will they convey any of the feelings I had in some fresh vital way? Or will they simply convey some vain human conceit or preoccupation? Surely art at its best is a form of worship and celebration. Otherwise, it fails as dismally as words.

2.VIII.86
SATURDAY

SPENT A RESTLESS NIGHT of very little sleep, even though I was provided with my own separate room. I missed the silence and peace of our camp. Here there were all kinds of noises all night long. Comings and goings.

Got up precisely at 7 AM out of habit of the last eight days ready to give my weather report. They served a hearty breakfast and I went with Hans to sort out the cans of supplies we had hastily packed. He will take the cans back and salvage whatever tinned food and supplies he can use next year.

We wandered over to the communications room to see Barry Hough, to return his maps and thank him profusely for all his kindness and patience and his advice for next year. His is a tremendous job of great pressure with everything going on here channelled through him. He suggested someone I should contact in Ottawa who could advise us about icebergs off the east coast.

We have confirmed that our flight departs at 5:35 PM. We eat too much here. Talk a great deal with the variety of people passing through. But Resolute should have been called Desolate for it has none of the qualities so special about the high Arctic.

Spend rest of the day wandering around, repacking, eating lunch, conversations until near takeoff time. Checked all our luggage and got our boarding passes. During day in Hudson's Bay Store, I meet a French Canadian who lives here and is married to an Inuit. He fishes and stocks his freezer. When he overhears me ask store clerk about buying an Arctic char and clerk's reply that they are sold out, he kindly offers to sell some of his own at $2/lb. Problem is to get it home frozen.

We take off in Pacific Western 737 for Cambridge Bay, then Yellowknife, where we have to leave plane with all our carry-on luggage to go through absurd security check. Finally arrive in Edmonton at 11 PM, or 10 PM their time, temperature is 24 degrees Celsius and it is dark—both of which seem strange to me. Go to nearby hotel and finally get to bed by 1 AM (12 AM their time). Although Jim and group want to meet for beer later on, I decline as I'm exhausted. In room am reluctant to turn on TV or look at newspaper and somehow want to savour the vision and feel of Ellesmere experience as long as possible before being inundated with all the comforts and confusions of civilized living.

In retrospect, the high Arctic distills or filters out through its great virgin spaces, stillness, magic light and spectacular beauty all the mundane and meaningless activities of one's daily living in the South and brings one into direct contact with an essential larger reality. It bestows a directness and simplicity, an earnestness and authenticity of sensation and reaction unencumbered by the complexities and distractions of modern life. My painting activity partook of this same directness of response to what I saw. The watercolours are like an embodiment, not literally but metaphorically, of the interaction. The encounter did something to me that only time can fully evaluate.

All the superficial comforts of this hotel seem sleazy and unreal. But I am tired, though exhilarated, not yet wanting to surrender Ellesmere.

3.VIII.86
SUNDAY

SLEPT SOUNDLY FOR eight hours. Had a hot shower. The first since leaving Saskatoon. My God, what a luxury. That is surely the first step to perdition, to corruption—modern plumbing! Cleanliness may not be so close to godliness and may be more aligned with ruin. Did it not have something to do with the fall of Rome? It is marvellous, but we forget the price we pay, and overvalue its importance.

So, I have come down now from God's country. Not quite Elysium because of the cold (although there is all the evidence of ancient tropical forests), yet there is something Edenic about it. One wonders, with just cause, will we have the wisdom to protect this land and the wildlife in it, or will we allow it to be exploited by tourism, hunting and fishing, commercial and industrial development and all that follows? When one sees the Inuit and First Nations and the deterioration of their way of life, the assault on their dignity, their separation from nature, and the many other visible inroads of modern culture, one cannot be hopeful that the Arctic will remain indefinitely wild and unspoiled.

If we do not value the Arctic with the muskox and the wolf and the caribou and allow all of this to vanish, we will have lost an invaluable guide not only to the way things were and what we have become, but more importantly, what we might yet be if we learn to live in harmony with and develop a reverence for this precious heritage, this primordial garden on the top of our planet.

Had Sunday brunch in hotel. The quantity and variety of food incredible—almost obscene when compared to being in the field and making do, and doing very well, on a limited diet. It reminds one strikingly of the wealth and abundance, the volume of waste in North America.

The airport with its piped-in muzak and fluorescent lights provides a synthetic cocoon, an environmental shroud that seems ugly and alien.

Civilization seems strange to me. I know I will, all too quickly, become part of it again but shall try to resist or slow down the process.

When I am asked about Ellesmere I find it difficult to talk about. Emotions well up in me and bring tears to my eyes which I can't fully explain. Like an innocence and intensity of experience that transcends culture, Ellesmere may fade from my memory but its essence will remain, I think, like a lodestar of hope and aspiration against which whatever I do will be measured.

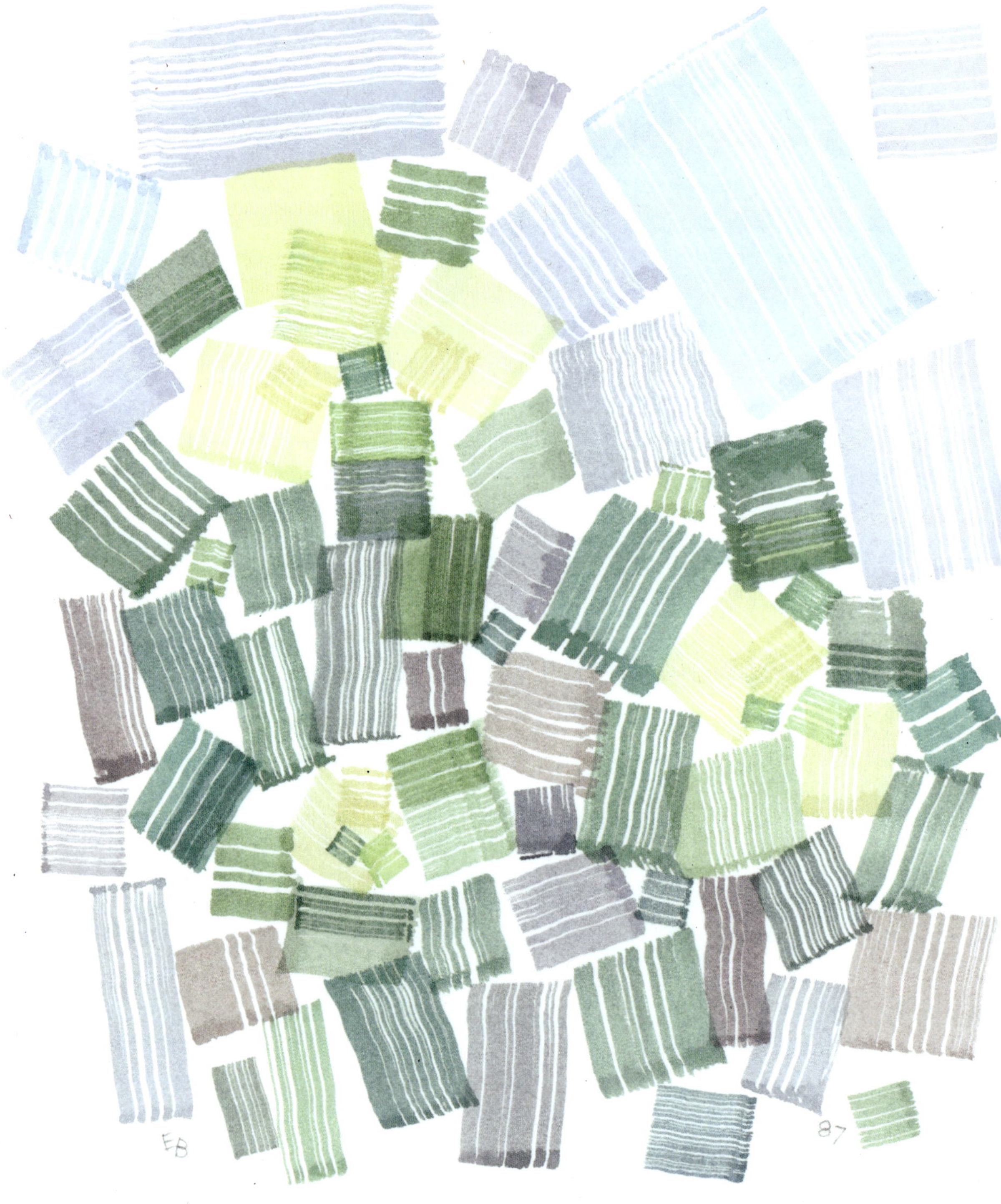
EB
87

ARCTIC JOURNALS

PART II | 1987

Arctic Study No. 47 | 1987
WATERCOLOUR ON PAPER, 25.4 × 20.3 CM
PRIVATE COLLECTION

4.VII.87

SATURDAY

IT IS ALMOST ONE YEAR since the first trip to Ellesmere. This is of course a celebrated day for America—the anniversary of their Declaration of Independence. On a more personal note, it is the day that I proposed marriage to Christina 22 years ago. It is also the day that Thoreau took up residence in the house he built on Walden Pond in 1845. I suspect his was a short but jubilant move for what proved to be a most renowned and productive year. Whereas I departed Saskatoon this morning rather bleary-eyed after a late night of last-minute packing for an early morning departure and very little sleep.

My inclination toward the North remains as intense as ever—like the needle on a compass. Yet I must admit some trepidation. I wonder whether the second experience will be as overwhelming as the first one. The freshness and intensity of first experiences are often not repeatable. Yet second or successive experiences and more familiarity—especially where art, people and places are concerned—can lead to further depth and richness. Although we are bound for Ellesmere via Resolute as last year, we plan to visit different parts of this incredible island and go to Alexandra Fjord and the east coast and explore that area in high hopes of seeing more icebergs. With some luck, we may even see some calving which we never observed last year. As well, we hope to spend a few days with Jim Basinger on Axel Heiberg Island to see the fossil forest there before moving on and settling in at Alexandra.

Flight to Edmonton short, with cold breakfast. Wait in airport here a long while, flight delayed because of some "paperwork" as the pilot explained. Take off for Yellowknife around 11 AM with boisterous fishing party aboard. Lunch finally served around 2 PM after we leave Yellowknife. Arrive at Resolute around 4 PM where temperature down to around 5 degrees Celsius with brisk south wind. We are met at airport by very pleasant man, Bob Christie, who explains we are to spend the night with him. Very shortly thereafter we are joined by Barry Hough, the base manager who we remember so well from last summer, who greets us and says he will be shipping us right out to Axel and that we should go over and have supper and plan to leave around 7 PM.

I find myself very cold with only my Saskatoon summer clothes on, so hasten to unpack in the nearby laundry room frantically searching for my long johns, turtleneck, wool sweater and parka. In short order, I emerge clothed for Resolute.

Despite the fact that we had lunch only two hours earlier, at 5 PM we have a hearty dinner. This may well be the last such fresh and elaborate meal we will have for the next three or four weeks. Some minor repacking and we anxiously wait to be called for flight.

Shortly before 7 PM we are informed that there is no room for us and our baggage on the flight and will have to spend the night here.

At first when we were told we were going right on to Axel we were disappointed, having looked forward to a leisurely evening of adjusting mentally and preparing for the next step. Then we quickly adjusted to the idea of leaving and getting on to Axel and seeing Jim. So, with this last-minute change we were again disappointed and particularly uncomfortable with the indefinite prospect of waiting to get out—God knows how many days now. This is so typical of travel in the North: uncertainty, changeability and the need for flexibility. "The best laid plans of mice and men" not only go astray here often, but the vicissitudes of weather—that ultimate and fickle power that determines movement so much in the North—and the availability of aircraft make it impossible to make or follow any rigid plans.

We are taken with all our gear to Bob's quarters, a kind of trailer that he uses as office and living quarters. There are three or four extra cots, table and chairs.

Before turning in, we decide to take a walk on a road leading north. While walking, low clouds move in and suddenly an enormous rainbow or parhelion arches over us that dissolves the buildings and barren hills. It is a marvellous reminder of the subtle, delicate quality of light that is so unique to the North. Arctic light can so quickly transform the drab desolateness of Resolute into a radiant paradise.

Return to our cots. Unpack sleeping bags. Bob is already asleep. Hans, bless his heart, zips up his bag and drops into a deep sleep. Despite my earplugs, I am resigned to getting little sleep. It is not only the snoring, but the bright light. For even though it is after 11 PM, it is as bright as noon.

5.VII.87

SUNDAY

AS ANTICIPATED, VERY LITTLE SLEEP, but despite yesterday's exhaustion, feel surprisingly good. Rise for breakfast, which is only available from 7 AM to 8 AM, and the dining room closes sharply at 8. The cook and general regime here is changed. Last year the cook was congenial and accommodating; this year it seems more like an army mess hall.

Went to see Barry around 10 AM and he informed us that we will be here until Monday afternoon. There is a film crew from Montreal also wanting to go to Axel to do a TV documentary of the ancient forest. All their camera equipment was lost and they are waiting for it. We will all go there together.

Since we are to spend the whole day here, Hans asked Barry if we could use the PCSP [Polar Continental Shelf Project] truck to drive to the Inuit village and see a little more of the vicinity. He kindly agrees, so we drove about both morning and afternoon.

Weather today exceedingly mild for Resolute: between 8 and 10 degrees Celsius, clear sunny sky. The only undesirable aspect was a constant wind of 30 to 40 miles per hour from the northeast.

At village, drove down to beach which was strewn with skidoos, sledges, boats, carcasses of seals, bones and various other refuse. Water still frozen with skidoos and sledges out on ice. String of six sled dogs tied up and baking in the sun. Hans busy shooting photos of morning mist lifting from bay with faint rainbow. I discover whale vertebrae. Later we walk back to another string of dogs. These not as large and more scrawny. Young girl playing with them. We talk. Her name is Mavis and she tells us which dog is the leader and shows us a newborn pup and places it by mother for nursing.

After lunch we drive to another part of the island and circle back toward village and drive out on grey gravel beach. Discover along this bleak coast a small cemetery of white wood markers, mostly Inuit graves piled over with gravel mounds since it is unlikely they could dig very deep into permafrost. There is one grave of a British pilot killed in an airplane crash at age 39, whose family thought he would want to be buried on Resolute to honour all "Arctic explorers and adventurers." This grave site is a sobering experience. Life and death in this harsh remote landscape seems to echo Koheleth or Solomon: "Vanity of vanities. All is vanity and the vexation of spirit."

Most of the crosses have fading remnants of Inuit writing. Several burial mounds have low white picket fences around them and a few have the odd artificial flowers or wreaths that the wind has not yet managed to remove. The artificial roses seem a poignant irony, almost an absurdity, compared to the overwhelming reality of this place and its utter isolation. Even the cross, not necessarily the sign of Christianity but of the presence of humankind, seems a very temporary marker soon to fall as others already have, and eventually to vanish. Somehow an Inuit artifact of any kind would have seemed more appropriate.

Out on the ice is a small iceberg, or more likely, the outcropping of pressure ice in a formation about 25 feet high of various peaks and valleys. The sun makes it glisten as if its interior were composed of diamonds and the light creates lovely blue shadows, haloes and translucent shades. Hans ignored the partly melted ice and before I know it is out around and within this stunning ice castle. I can see he has become obsessed with it and lost all track of time. There are sure to be some fine photographs.

Back to PCSP for wash-up and dinner.

The latest word is that we may leave early tomorrow morning as Barry wrestles with the complexities of the many expeditions scattered across the Arctic and responds to all the different needs. We shall see.

After meal, return to trailer and decide to take an evening walk. The water's edge, in view west of us, seems like a reasonable destination. We are once again completely fooled. As we had learned last year, and had now forgotten, distances here are misleading. It turns out to be over three miles each way over torturous rock. I have never seen such rock formations—like stratified or striated layers that are seen on cliffs or walls but not on the ground. These have been broken and moved by ice and water to form very rugged and sharp surfaces. Upon nearing the beach, I sight a heroic clump of saxifrage in all its purple glory surrounded by expanses of grey pebbles stretching as far as one can see to the frozen water. Returning against the relentless wind is hard work. We console ourselves with the thought that it is good training for things to come. That sleeping bag will surely feel good tonight.

6.VII.87
MONDAY

WE ARE DEFINITELY LEAVING this morning. After breakfast we are issued our radio and rifle which must be signed out. We pack all our things and are picked up by truck to begin loading plane.

Pilot of the plane is the same one who took us to Otto Fjord last year. Doug remembers us. He is very gentle, soft-spoken, tall, 40ish. We are in good hands.

Because the film crew of five who are also going to Axel Heiberg have so much equipment, including gasoline generators for lights, there is concern that there is too much weight with all of us (nine passengers, including pilot and co-pilot, and all our baggage and equipment) for the Otter to take off. We are approached by Barry who questions why we have so much stuff. We explain that we have essentially the same as last year. Barry remains tense, somewhat agitated, and we are disturbed by his insinuations. Both Hans and I offer to eliminate various items to lighten the load. But by now the plane is already packed to its limit and before we know it we are all asked to board the plane through the cockpit and squeeze into every available seat.

We are tense because of all the previous concerns about weight, so takeoff becomes an anxious experience. But Doug lifts off the runway beautifully and we are airborne and on our way. Somehow it is an emotion-filled experience that revives one's faith in humankind's inventiveness, the power he has achieved through his incredible machines. Surely the human mind is one of nature's great creations.

We wondered what all the fuss was about. If there was a genuine concern about too much weight, why did they not remove the tents and heater and kerosene drum we suggested be left behind? If there wasn't a real problem then why make such a disturbance over nothing? To say the least, we are baffled by Barry's unexplained behaviour.

The flight is about three and a half hours long and the views of the land and sea we pass over are spectacular.

We land in a valley dotted with tents—about 20. There are numerous other people here—most attracted by the fossil forest nearby.

Jim is not present, but away with colleagues on a long hike to another valley. We move all our gear to a location suggested for us and spend some time setting up our Logan tents.

Temperature here is in the 20s [Celsius]—incredibly warm and warmer than we ever experienced last year. As a consequence there are hordes of mosquitoes. We cover our faces and hands with repellent that seems to hold them at bay—temporarily anyways. However, their presence in such numbers remains a nuisance, also not encountered last year.

We are surprised to see so many people. I put aside immediately any possibility of painting while here, which, in any case, is to be for only a few days. I know that I require solitude to work and think. I do not function well nor am I at my best in groups, congenial as they may be.

Jane, an Australian geologist working with Jim, invites us to join the film crew on a tour of the fossil forest site. As part of this entourage we proceed to climb the mountain. The group becomes scattered with attention focused on the forthcoming film. Hans and I eventually leave to explore the terrain by ourselves.

There is something about photography, photographers, filmmaking and filmmakers that is abhorrent and obnoxious. I think it is the notion that everything is grist for their camera to be snapped or shot, consumed or disposed of. Here on this sacred site where silence, and perhaps prayer or at least awe, would seem most appropriate, the image-makers and their image machines shoot everything in sight. There is something basically wrong. What should be a religious and deeply humbling experience becomes mere material for entertainment. The formation of these fossil forests took many millions of years. The film crew and photography deals with it in a few moments or days. Imagine Charles Darwin with a film crew in his backyard, with floodlights and tape recorders following him about!

Despite all the people, the site is spectacular with various tree trunks excavated and exposed. The peak or ridge of this mountain where we are was once a valley that became a riverbed when the forest was eventually covered over by silt and sand.

There is an earnestness and rightness about the herd of muskox we see grazing some ten miles away across a great green river valley below. Our presence seems an irreverent intrusion.

We hike back to our camp in the valley to finish erecting our tents and sorting out our belongings.

Since our food supply destined for Axel was mistakenly forwarded directly to Alexandra Fjord, we are to be guests here. We will eat in the large cook tent that they call the "Geodetic Hilton."

Also, we are not required to set up our radio here or call in, something we will have to do at Alexandra.

We dine together with a number of people. Help with the dishes and get ourselves ready for bed. The temperature drops around 10 PM and it gets cold. Fortunately, this eliminated the mosquitoes.

7.VII.87

TUESDAY

AFTER BREAKFAST AND MEETING with Jim, we take another tour of the fossil forest with Jim's student, Ben, who explains many things and takes us to other sights we hadn't seen yesterday. We gather a few samples of the different kinds of fossil wood as well as amber and pine cones.

These ancient stumps are metasequoia or dawn sequoia trees, to which present living sequoia are distantly related. Ben explains the different processes of fossilization:

Mineralization—where trees become petrified like rock
Carbonization—where the final result is coal
Mummification—where much of the original character is preserved

The uniqueness of much of this fossil forest is that the remains are mummified.

The successive layers of forest are separated by millions of years between the extinction of one forest and the beginning and maturation of the next on the same site with deposits of silt, sand and soil between them. These dark rings of fossilized forest on the mountains appear on each side of the valley or on continuous ranges. There are as many as ten or more rings visible.

I have said that the human mind is one of nature's great creations. However, here on Axel Heiberg, when one is in the presence of this 45-million-year-old fossil forest and sees how nature has made mountains into rivers, rivers into mountains, transformed lush tropics into arid desert and stacked forest upon forest through great stretches of time, the power of the human mind shrinks and recedes accordingly as scientists continue to grapple and disagree upon how to fully explain all that has transpired on this earth.

In the afternoon, Ben agrees to take us through some valleys where we might see some muskox and possibly find some muskox skulls. There are a number to be seen in camp—one beautiful specimen for the national museum in Ottawa.

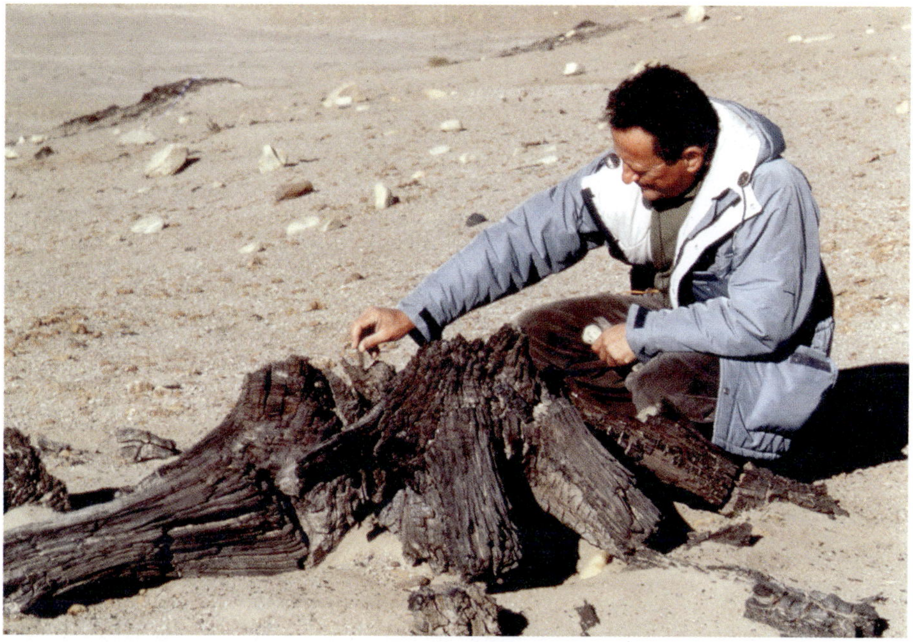

HANS DOMMASCH, **Eli beside Petrified Wood, Axel Heiberg Island** | 1987

After walking for about three miles (we had already walked four or five in the morning) my arthritic back began to bother me and I could see I would only slow them down and that it would become increasingly painful to continue the full circuit of ten or 12 miles. So, I suggest that they proceed without me and I return to camp at my leisure.

Do my back exercises, which I haven't done since leaving Saskatoon, and various other chores.

Hans and Ben return to camp four hours later; they have had an interesting encounter with some muskox. They return with a nice, well-aged skull. (I suggest Hans mount this on his office door, which might serve to reduce complaints or foolish requests in his department.)

The party of paleontologists or paleobiologists return triumphant because they discovered some bones today, including that of a turtle and other animals. As a consequence we learn that this party, which includes Mary Dawson, will stay a few more days to do some sifting for more bones. As we are to fly out with them, our departure is now scheduled for Friday.

8.VII.87
WEDNESDAY

HELICOPTER TAKES BEN, HANS AND ME to the glacier nearby from which we will hike back seven or eight miles. My first helicopter ride, quite exciting, lasting only about ten minutes (while our return walk will take us around four or five hours including a stop for lunch overlooking the great glacier on one side and the wide riverbed on the other).

Encounter two different sets of muskox. A male and female in each case, and have a very good look at them. Hans shoots several rolls of film. In one instance the male, who is large with a luxurious coat of regal fur, warns us off by pawing the ground and rubbing his nose across his left leg. Magnificent creatures who truly are kings of this domain. They regard us with suspicion and caution before proceeding. We are curious and not particularly welcome intruders. This ancient animal, who is said to be the only one that survived the ice age, requires vigilant protection before increasing visitors, poachers and trophy hunters become a more serious threat to its future. Surviving the ice age is one thing, surviving humans is quite another!

Seeing the fossil forest and the glacier reminds me that one of the most profound Arctic shocks is that confrontation between human time and geological time. Our minute human lifespan can hardly relate to the millions of years involved in the processes of fossilization and formation of mountains and glaciers. A related phenomenon is that one's sense of time in the Arctic slows down. It decelerates and points out the absurdity of haste in daily life. The natural rhythms of time—the movement of the Earth around the sun and the seasons—become far more important than all the hectic schedules and deadlines of daily civilized life. One consequence of Arctic time is that one learns patience, since one is surrounded by all these great changes occurring over such long stretches of time. Modern humans, of course, tend increasingly to ignore geology and the wisdom of the earth.

Another Arctic shock is scale. Human size is so small, so insignificant, in relation to the great space and distance here. So much that one sees and experiences here, in fact, overwhelms and leaves one speechless. Yet, why do I scribble in my journal, paint, photograph in response? Perhaps because one is so awestruck by such magnitudes of time and space, light, and above all, beauty. One is made to feel so inconsequential yet simultaneously made to forget one's self; one's self-centredness and self-pity vanishes. Perhaps in some way one's art—be it writing, painting or photography—becomes an act of worship or prayer in recognition of this immense process of which one is such a very momentary part. We become a thinking part like Pascal's "thinking reed." Our art may also be a defiant response to our brief mortality and eventual fossilization and oblivion.

9.VII.87

THURSDAY

THIS MORNING WENT with Jim and Jane up to fossil forest. Jim wants Hans to photograph various sites including him and Jane working. There are slides and photos needed for lecturing and publishing. He asks me to take some black and whites with my larger format Bronica for use in publication where colour is not possible.

While they are shooting, I wander about to gather amber stones or nuggets. As it happens, my name as my father pronounced it is Baernstein which in German means amber stone. Since my father could not speak English when he came to America around 1905, the immigration authorities at Ellis Island spelled it the closest or easiest way it occurred to them. Thus Born instead of Baern.

The resin of these ancient fossil trees was subject to the same pressure and processes, gradually being transformed into amber. Some of the smaller pieces are more crystal clear. Larger pieces more milky and opaque yellow. The natural gold of this Arctic amber often catches the light and sparkles like a gemstone

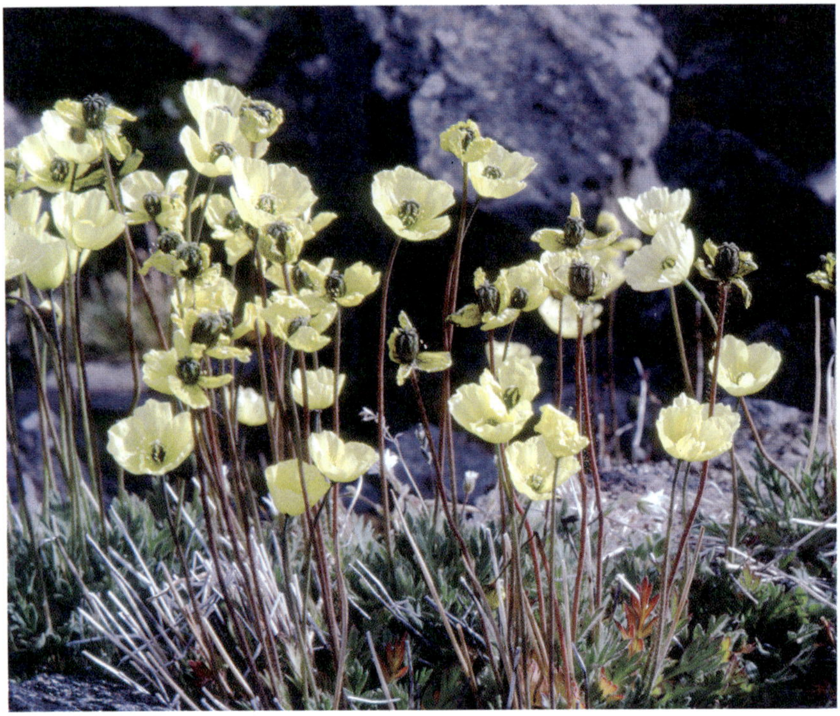

HANS DOMMASCH, **Arctic Poppy** | 1987

amidst the compressed black and grey layers of leaves and branches and cones. A lovely sight indeed.

Later Jim and Jane show us how to sift through the black layers of leafy compressed matter imbedded in the hillsides to find metasequoia cones. Although trees were estimated to be up to 100 feet tall, like the California sequoia, their cones are not very large—somewhere between the size of a nickel and quarter in diameter.

After a good lunch and return to the camp, Hans and I take a hike around behind one of the mountains on the southwest side of the valley in which the base camp is situated. We follow an old rocky riverbed that winds up gradually into a wide green pasture or meadow residing in what are otherwise such arid looking mountains, with some appearing almost like great sand pyramids.

As I walk I suddenly notice at my feet between the clumps of grass-covered earth a small butterfly almost one-third the size of a monarch with similar though different colour and finer markings as its wings are spread facing the sun. As soon as the sun goes behind a cloud the wings are quickly brought together to conserve heat. So many things here are extremely light and heat sensitive. The Arctic poppies, because of the short summer season, follow the sun all day and night long like a receiver dish tracking the course of the sun.

Ben told us of an Arctic butterfly that takes 13 years to go through the metamorphosis from caterpillar to butterfly. I wonder if this was one of them.

After dinner in the communal cook tent packed with 20 people, we take our usual evening walk before bed. Hard to believe it is 11 PM with the light and sun in the northwest. The light seems lower than in the middle of the day, and as it is reflected in the stream nearby it looks and feels more like early morning after sunrise.

Stop in at cook tent on the way back. Jim has brought out a bottle of Glenfiddich that he was saving for a special occasion, and we have a drink before turning in.

10.VII.87

FRIDAY

WHEN I WAKE around 7:30 AM and emerge from my tent, I notice that my towel, which I left tied to the stake rope last night, is about 15 feet away lying all rolled up in the dirt. I figure there must have been a terrific wind last night that managed to untie my towel.

At breakfast in the cook tent, Dave tells me that early this morning around 4 AM there were four wolves in the camp. He saw one of them, a younger one, take my towel and play with it, rolling in it. They evidently stayed for a while fascinated by all the strange things here, and then left. It is amazing that they did not go into the cook tent that is filled with food of all kinds, or some of the other tents that also have food. Dave suggests that the strong smell of my towel must have been very attractive! So much for the myth about the aggressive viciousness of wolves.

We are scheduled to leave Axel today but Jim reports that Barry says present weather in Alexandra Fjord is bad. Must wait and see. Plane to arrive at around 1 PM. Call Barry who confirms plane's arrival and that we could go as far as Eureka if weather doesn't improve, but that there are signs of it clearing.

Another party is also going out, composed of Mary Dawson, a well-known paleontologist; Cliff Morrow, a Carnegie Museum artist; and two other scientists. They are bound for Bay Fjord where they discovered the skull of a flying lemur last year. They have a large quantity of gear.

We proceed to dismantle our tents and pack. It is cold and windy.

Twin Otter finally arrives in our valley. Since there is so much to move out and little room to take off, the pilot decides he will take Mary's party and their stuff out first as far as Eureka and then come back for us, go back to Eureka and pick them up and fly to Bay Fjord first and then to Alexandra.

We say our goodbyes when the Otter comes back for us and make our way to Eureka. We help load the plane while it refuels in Eureka, and with a full load, take off. Bay Fjord is an incredible looking place with red hills and pale olive-green valleys and pastures. The red earth is reminiscent of Prince Edward Island, but the geologist explains that it is quite different. Evidently, these hills were all coal some thousands or millions of years ago and probably the lightning struck and started an enormous fire that baked all the clay so that the red is like first clay broken into gravel. The delicate moss green against this brick or flowerpot clay is a most moving sight.

The pilot lands his plane on the rising slope of the mountain, coming to a stop almost at the summit. After helping with the unloading, they discover that their radio transmitter has been left by mistake in Eureka. Fortunately, they have a spare one, but one that doesn't operate on the same frequency. After some involved calling-in by the pilot and temporary adjustments they discover they can communicate, with some difficulty, but it will serve them until another one can be brought in a few days. Mary Dawson, who looks like someone's lovable grandmother, seems quite calm and unruffled by all these confused happenings. She is obviously in tune with geological time.

I could not help but reflect upon how such paleontologists, paleobiologists, paleobotanists and geologists render time transparent. They slowly reveal more of the vast invisible past by their careful sifting and searching for remains of ancient flora and fauna, animal skeletons and remnants of the earth's evolution. Similarly, archaeology and anthropology render the cultural past visible, revealing the presence and movements of prehistoric man. These patient fossil hunters allow us to peer through great spans of opaque time, rendering it increasingly more transparent. They are largely unsung heroes who significantly enlarge and transform our vision.

We take off going down the mountain and, with all these flights, I continue to marvel at the wonders of these incredible airplanes and pilots. The one-hour flight to Alexandra is through some of the most spectacular country I have ever seen. We fly over dozens of glaciers, canyons and gorges of unbelievable shapes, sizes and colours. In one instance, the white tongue of a glacier comes down to the edge of jade green water of the fjord. The scale and varieties of the mountain architecture are forever changing. Rivers run through deep gorges with all manner of eroded spires and buttresses. There are emerald-coloured pools and lakes, and others malachite green. This flight alone will have made this Arctic trip worthwhile. It occurs to me that I can never live long enough to see and follow every river, canyon, gorge, glacier and mountain in this incredible land, and I feel a great sense of loss.

Before we know it, the pilot puts us down at Alexandra Fjord where we are surprised to see a number of simple white-painted buildings. This is an abandoned RCMP post, and we have been told we can stay inside one of the buildings.

We unload the plane, chat with Karl, the pilot, and after the Otter takes off we look around at our new location, our base for the next 20 days. The buildings are near the water, facing some islands and Thorvald Peninsula across the fjord. In the distance about ten miles away is Bache Peninsula. Behind and around us are dark brown mountains with several large glaciers in the distance.

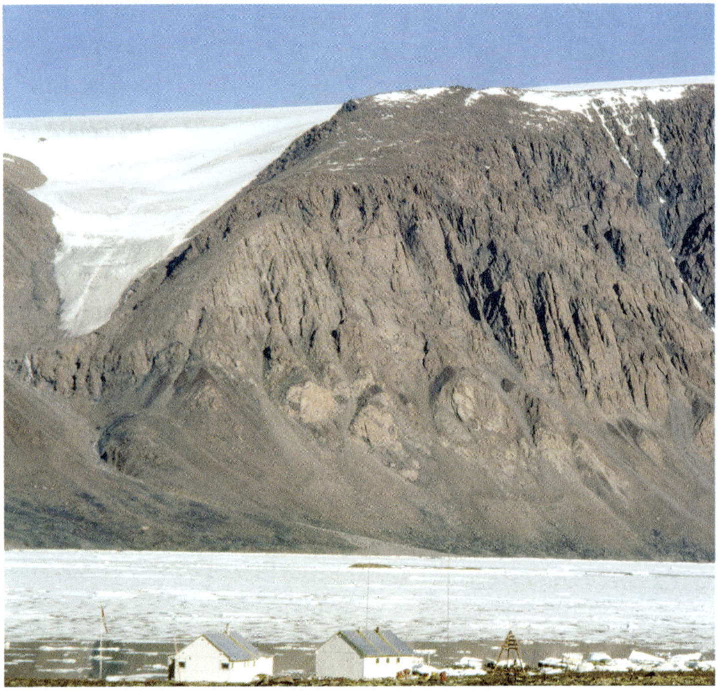

HANS DOMMASCH, **Abandoned RCMP Post, Alexandra Fjord** | 1987

We note that all our pails of food are at one side of the runway, left there for us about a month ago.

Decide to walk down to the buildings in the hope that someone may have left the key for us to get in. All buildings are locked with a sturdy brass padlock. It is raining slightly and one can feel the dampness (especially as compared to Axel). We are faced with a dilemma. Should we put up our tents (and where) in the hope of getting the key in the next few days or should we try to get into one of the buildings where it will be dry and we can cook our meals and sleep, and generally be much more comfortable and freer to pursue our interests? We notice that by removing two screws the hasp on one of the doors would be disconnected and we could open the door. Do we have a substantial screwdriver? Fortunately, Hans has had the good sense to pack one in his camera bag. We have some difficulty making the decision to remove the two screws. Visions loom of our being charged with breaking and entering an RCMP post! Yet we have been told we could stay there and the key would be made available. But with all the red tape and confused lines of communication, here we are at 7:30 PM with our pile of gear and without the key. For better or for worse, even if it means some harsh confrontation with Renfrew, or some admonitions from Barry, we agree I should remove the two screws. This done, we enter the building that has all and more than we require.

Over the next few hours we hastily have some food and proceed to set up our radio and antenna. After some trial and error (we have forgotten from last year) all is in order so I call in about 9:30 PM to let them know we are here and communication is established loud and clear.

Next item of business is to find fresh water. We have heard what sounded like a waterfall in the distance and expect it is likely on the other side of the mountain. To our surprise, after walking about we find a roaring, deeply cut river coming from the glacier into the fjord about a quarter of a mile away. The water is cold, clear and delicious. So, our water supply is established.

Being so close to water and glacier it is cool and damp here. The dampness especially gets to me. The buildings are also quite cool and damp. As we are tired and it is almost midnight and will have to get up at 6:30 AM for the morning weather report, we retire into our respective bedrooms putting our mattress and sleeping bag on one of the numerous beds available. Each new place one comes to has a strangeness and even eeriness about it until one gradually comes to know it better.

11.VII.87
SATURDAY

THIS RCMP POST which we are inhabiting is sparsely furnished but quite spacious and has been, and obviously is still being, used by others in the vicinity. Peter Schledermann has a group of around nine, we were told, across from here on Skraeling Island. I believe he is an archaeologist and there is an old Viking site they are excavating and making a documentary film about.

There is a sink here but no running water. A large wood or coal burning stove but no wood. Electric light fixtures but no electricity. And a gas cooking and baking range, but no gas. So, we have brought in all our supplies including the Coleman stove and live as we did in our tent except with much more space.

Around 10 AM a helicopter lands on the bay in front of us to get fuel. Several people can be seen approaching our place. They are army officers from Eureka doing research in the area—surveying and mapping. They ask what we are doing here, who we are, how we got into the building, etc. We explain everything and are asked to write down our names. They seem to understand and accept the situation, although it is pointed out that we should normally have been given a key and properly signed for it with the RCMP. Someone at Resolute has not done things properly.

The officer in charge writes down his name and frequency where he can be reached and says to look him up if we get back to Eureka, and we can have a beer together. We are relieved.

After lunch we go for a hike with cameras following the river toward its source, the glacier. Take photographs of the water and rocks. The roaring noise

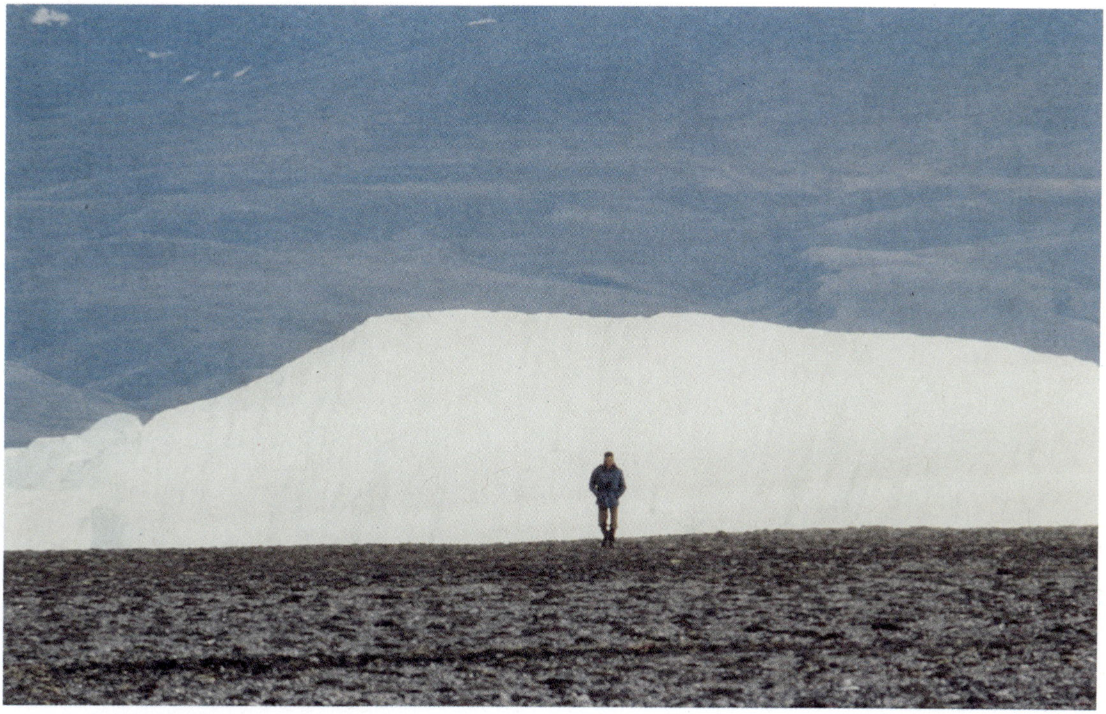

HANS DOMMASCH, **Eli Bornstein** | 1986 or 1987

we have been hearing proves to be a 15-to-20-foot waterfall in a gorge. What is it that is so frightening, so terrifying about a waterfall? Is it the sheer power, the blind force of its movement?

Air still cool, around 6 degrees Celsius at 6 PM with north wind. Scattered clouds with sun occasionally breaking through to light up distant mountains and glacier.

Today, discover a cairn with a bronze plaque about an eighth of a mile away from our building. It is dedicated to A.Y. Jackson, who first painted here in 1927. I am, in fact, reminded of his paintings by the brown mountains, the buildings here on the slope down to the fjord, and all the broken ice. The cairn was pointed out to us by the army captain after I mentioned that I am an artist hoping to do some painting here.

There is much about this place that is very scenic in a picture postcard or calendar sense. The weathered white houses against the mountains, the glaciers, the fjord, all have been seen too often. Yet there is a kind of dark and sombre, brooding beauty about this place, particularly when the sky is overcast and the mountains loom on all sides. They are dark browns, oranges and mauves.

I expected something quite different. I expected to be near the open sea and of course icebergs. We are quite a way from the open water opposite Greenland. Here the fjord is still frozen over with melting and breaking up near the shore. The swollen rivers from the glaciers run into the fjord and the tides rise and fall, alternately lifting up the huge ice chunks and dropping them again.

After supper (of beans and bacon) we decide to bring in our kerosene heater and try to heat up the kitchen. This proves to be more complicated than anticipated, and takes over two hours to get it going properly. They forgot to give us a funnel among other things. Go to bed far later than planned.

12.VII.87

SUNDAY

HANS GETS UP at 5 AM to do some shooting in the morning light with the sun lower and longer shadows. After breakfast, unpack my paints and make my way down to a lovely pond. In the process, the new shoulder strap on my new paint box breaks and the box hits the rocks so hard one of the hinges on the cover breaks off with the splintered wood. The mosquitoes next join the fracas and my new folding stool sinks in the sediment! Despite all these minor disasters, I proceed to paint first watercolour. Must come back tomorrow to try it again.

After lunch, with the sun shining and the temperature now up to 21 degrees Celsius, we decide to hike eastward out to a point where we might get a glimpse of the ocean sea. Get as far as the second river which is so fast and deep we can't find any place where we can possibly cross where the water would not be over the tops of our rubber boots. So, we turn back and wander along the shore on the ice, and photograph some of the beautiful reflections and transparencies

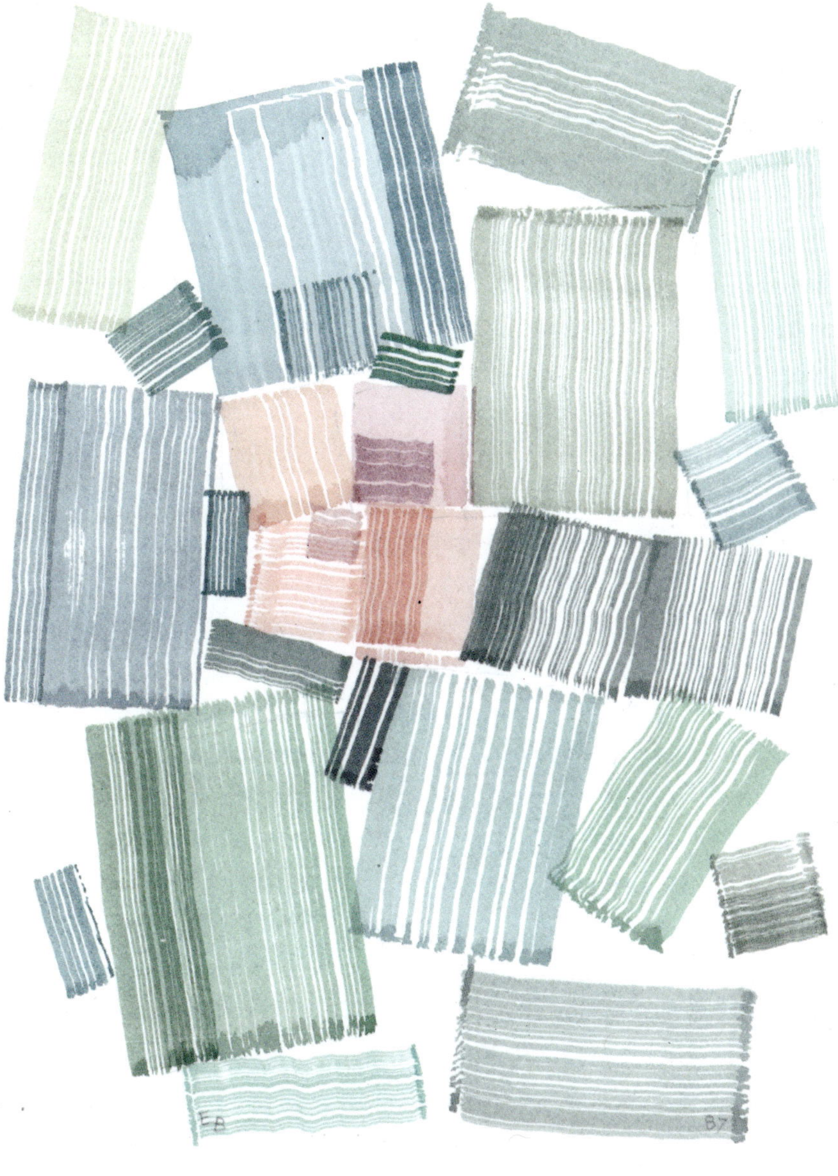

Arctic Study No. 34 | 1987

WATERCOLOUR ON RAG BOARD, 25 × 20 CM PRIVATE COLLECTION

to be seen all around. Climb over the huge chunks of ice and slowly and often precariously make our way back. The warmth of the sun is a great joy.

13.VII.87
MONDAY

WEATHER COLD. Down to around 7 degrees Celsius and completely overcast. Spend the morning doing odd jobs like repairing my broken paint box. Decide that after lunch we will hike to the west toward the head of the fjord that we cannot see from here. Meanwhile, army helicopter lands on bay below us to refuel. We hasten down to see them to ask them to mail our letters, which they gladly agree to do.

We discover on our hike that most of the land approaching the mountains around us is more like a bog made up of muskeg with grass and rock. As one proceeds up the mountain, this condition prevails but is interspersed with larger rocks. Often it is rather swampy with many mosquitoes. The mosquitoes swarm around one and light upon one's clothes, face and hands but bite only occasionally—thank goodness. But they are a nuisance, yet I dislike using the repellent, which has a disagreeable smell, and makes one feel clammy, and as a dangerous poison, can't be too good for one's skin, I'm sure.

The mountains here, very unlike those at Axel Heiberg and Otto Fjord, are very rocky and inaccessible. The hike proves anything but enjoyable and is tough going. After about an hour and a half we stop to rest. Hans decides to scale the mountain to try to walk on the ridge or summit, which may be easier going. He says he will try it and let me know how it goes. After a while, as I don't hear from Hans, I take up and follow in his direction and finally spot him in the rocky incline and let him know I am going back, as the hike is neither pleasant nor the scenery particularly worthy of all the effort. Hans seems to have heard me, but shouts back he'll see me later. I make my way back through the bog and note that there is very little sign of animal life here, less than there was at Axel and Otto. Understandably so, since it is so much less inviting or accessible.

This place is a disappointment. Besides the fact that we are still far from the open sea on the east coast and there are no icebergs here, we seem to be hemmed in with the impassable rivers to the east of us, and then muskeg and rocky inaccessible mountain slope to our west, the fjord at our front and the glaciers and mountain behind us.

We need to get a helicopter to take us south and east along the coast and I shall be talking to Barry tonight about the soonest likelihood.

If the weather is sunny I can go back to my pond to paint the stunning reflections of the mountains and glacier across the fjord. So, I hope for sun tomorrow morning or at least a few more days of encounter with that lovely pool, which could occupy me for many a sunny day. While totally different from my "Moby" iceberg at Otto last year, this pond has the same kind of continuous or unending appeal as a source of ideas or approaches.

If the weather stays overcast, I would not like to stay here too much longer, as it becomes oppressive. Somehow all the relative comfort and ease provided by our staying in the RCMP post instead of a tent does not compensate for the limitations and restricted mobility of this place.

14.VII.87

TUESDAY

TALKED TO BARRY LAST NIGHT and he was favourable to my request for a helicopter to take us down the coast in search of icebergs. One pilot I asked about icebergs suggested Talbot Inlet, about 60 miles southeast; another suggested Cadogan Inlet, about 40 or 50 miles southeast.

This morning, Barry confirmed that a helicopter will pick us up around 1 PM, take us out to where we want to be put down and then after completing several other trips coordinated with other groups in this area, will come back to pick us up and take us back to Alexandra. Barry recommends that we take our tent and radio, as well as food as a safety precaution just in case there are any delays or changes of weather.

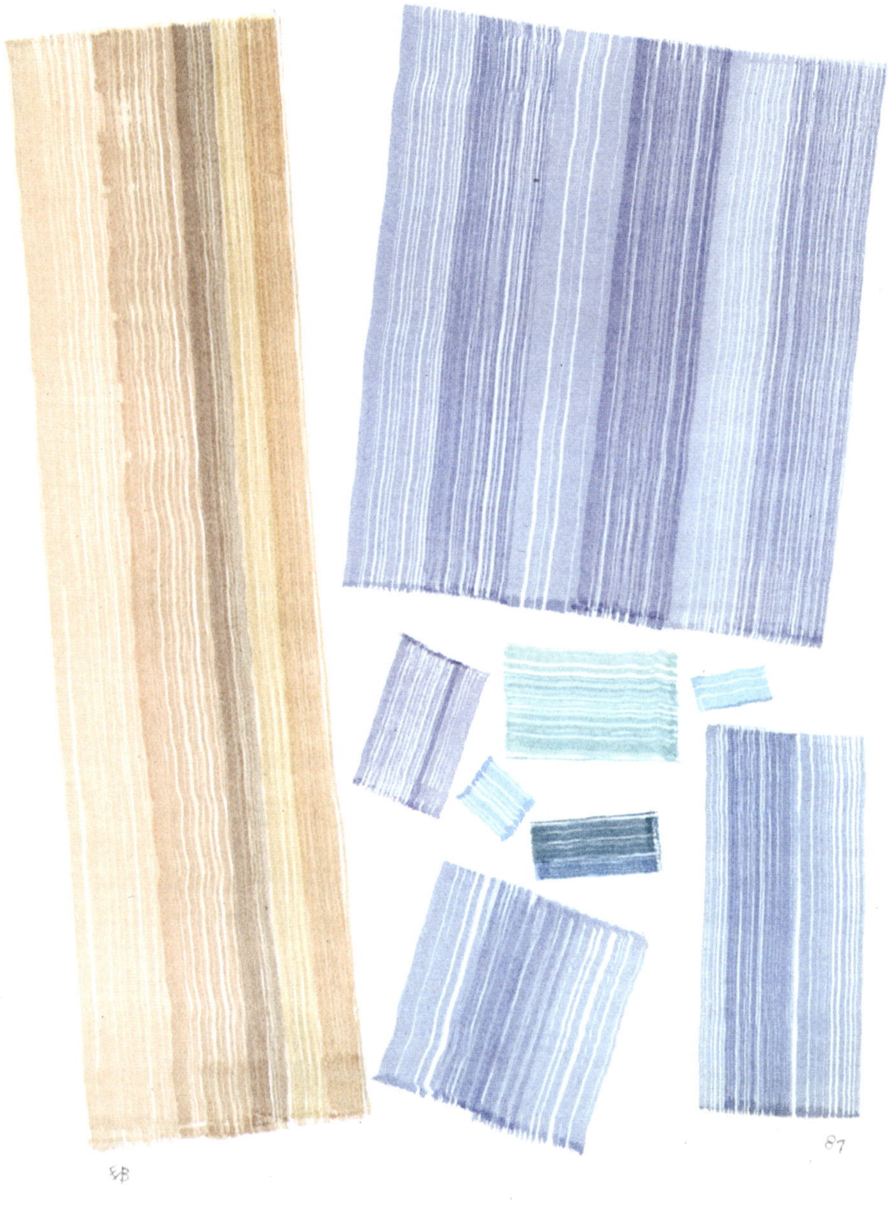

Arctic Study No. 35 | 1987 WATERCOLOUR ON RAG BOARD, 25.4 × 20.3 CM

So, we must pack for all eventualities. Will we at long last actually be seeing the open water of Baffin Bay, Greenland, some large icebergs and even some calving?

Sky is still largely overcast, temperature around 7 degrees Celsius, no wind, with some break and a bit of blue appearing in the west.

Here in the Arctic a great deal of time is spent just waiting. Waiting for the weather to change, waiting for the radio contact and coordination of movement, waiting for availability of airplanes. And with all this waiting there is always the uncertainty about what one will be able to do.

At 2 PM the helicopter arrives. The pilot is Chinese or Vietnamese and his name is Lin. He is very casual and friendly, but his English is hard to understand. When I call Barry to let him know we are leaving, he asks to speak to Lin and we discover that the radio in the helicopter is not working. Barry asks us to take our radio and call when we are put down, giving coordinates so he knows exactly where we are. We load up our gear including 20 or 30 mosquitoes and take off.

I wonder in the excitement of our first sighting of the open sea: will we at least see the icebergs I have been pursuing now for two summers? Or are the icebergs, like Captain Ahab's white whale, forever elusive—a figment or obsession of my imagination? From icebergs we have already seen, my anticipations and expectation would seem to have some basis in reality. I ponder, how can an iceberg, which is the epitome of coldness, emit such radiant light and beauty?

It is a great thrill to ride in these marvellous man-made birds. Once we are on the coast over the water Lin points out whales in the water and circles back, tilting sharply, to have another look. The sea and ice are interesting to look at as we pass over rocky terrain with the greatest ease. We fly for about 30 minutes before Lin puts us down on Wade Point near a vast glacier and many different-sized glaciers. It is quite exciting and reminiscent of Otto Fjord but it is a wilder area with great stretches of blue water as far as the eye can see to Greenland. Mountains are very rocky and rugged. Lin takes off and will come back to pick us up at around 8 PM. We set up radio and call Barry giving him our location: 78.33°N, 74.58°W.

Spend afternoon looking, taking photographs and sketching. I find it frustrating since distances are so great and I do not have a telephoto lens. Fortunately, Hans has, including an 800mm that brings the icebergs very close. With painting here it is equally frustrating as the light continues to change. I end up making sketches in pencil and notes I hope can be translated. Paintings in my mind's eye are magnificent. Getting them on paper is another matter entirely. There will be much struggling there to translate the qualities of the fresh colour sensations that I see all around, not literally, but into something else—not photographs or realistic descriptions. How to make a watercolour emanate some of the colour and light glowing all around one? That is the challenge: to put colour down in a uniquely abstract way that evokes sensations without imitating appearances, that has a life of its own, yet bears some indirect reference or relationship to what one has seen. Too much painting and photography have trivialized the Arctic with hackneyed and banal representations. Cliché and triteness result, while empty abstractions are just as boring.

A thought has often occurred to me, particularly when listening to or reading what artists say or write about their work. So much art today is essentially solipsistic: preoccupied with itself, measured only by itself, taking itself as the only reality and referring to nothing larger than itself. So many artists seem to embrace solipsism (as well as commercial success) as their credo. Art, no longer to the glory of God, is neither to the glory of nature nor humans. It is to the glory of itself—or art for art's sake at its very worst.

I try to find a brushstroke that is neutral or non-descriptive, varying it in size and shape or length and direction that will allow for a construction in which the colour panes can function in relationship to the space in a non-literal way. Yet the colour does have its source in nature and what I see. Even the construction is suggested to me from the Arctic in a very simplified or abstracted manner as the impetus for the generation of these watercolour studies.

The word abstract remains difficult. Yet one is stuck with the term through general or historical usage to distinguish it from realism or literal representation. For me, Arctic space/light/colour/form remain both real and abstract.

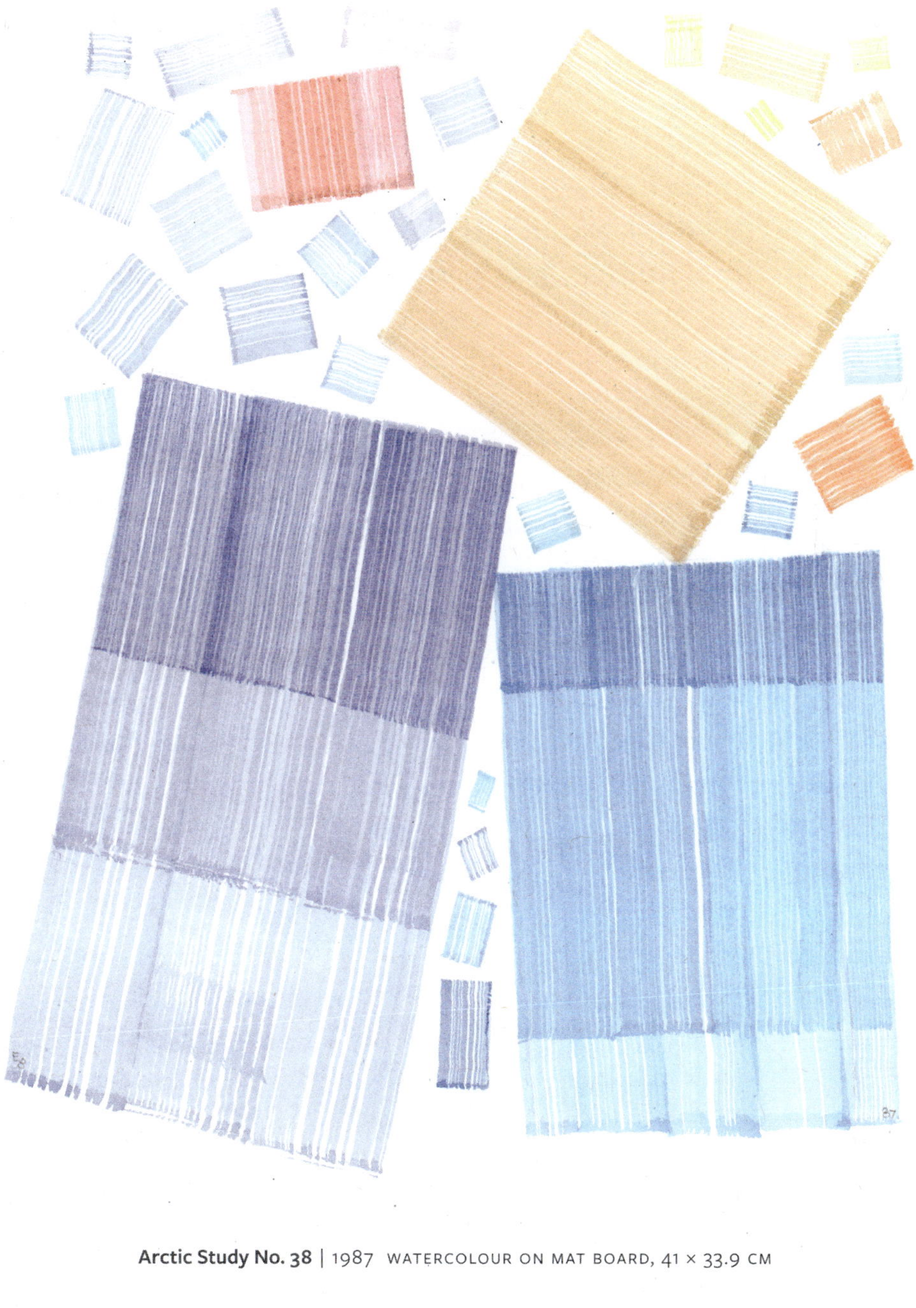

Arctic Study No. 38 | 1987 WATERCOLOUR ON MAT BOARD, 41 × 33.9 CM

There is an overwhelming purity of clarity of these elements here that make them at once abstract as well as real. My little studies will appear to many (often regrettably and apologetically) as abstract. To some others they may even appear as realistic. They are in fact neither or both, which only demonstrates how utterly inadequate, if not useless, such words and modes of perception have become.

As we wander about Wade Point we come upon the remains of an old Inuit settlement down by the rocky shore facing the glacier. Here there are the stone foundations of five or six dwellings, all circular, with the remaining walls about two or three feet high. One of the dwellings seems to have been the cooking or butchering place since there are still numerous very old and well-bleached bones from whales, walruses and other animals. One wonders what stories lie unrecorded of their lives here on the very easterly edge of Ellesmere Island, about 50 miles across from Greenland. What happy and what tragic times occurred on this spot? What courage and determination? We shall never know.

Lin arrives around 8:15 PM to pick us up. After calling Barry to let him know, we dismantle the radio and load our gear on the helicopter. This time I sit in the front seat of the Plexiglas bubble next to the pilot. Surely this is as close as one can get to flying like a bird. We fly out to look at the largest iceberg in the water and then back over Alfred Newton Glacier and the broken spires of ice being pushed forward and out to eventually calve in the water. There are spots of deep blue-green ice between some of the white pinnacles. The huge tongue of the glacier itself has the look of the skin of an enormous white whale with similar markings and texture that Melville described.

As we fly back, Lin points out a pod of whales playing in the open water. What a sight.

We learn that many of the place names here are not commemorative of explorers and discoverers but, contrary to my expectation, honoured wealthy brewers or merchants who may have sponsored expeditions. Places were also named for royalty or politicians who never set foot in the Arctic. Axel Heiberg, we are told, was such a brewer or politician as was Amund Ringnes in Norway.

Once back to Alexandra, we set up the radio again and call Barry. Finally to bed exhausted but exhilarated.

15.VII.87

WEDNESDAY

BARRY INFORMED US last night that because of a backlog of people waiting for the helicopter it may be some while before we can get it again.

We want very badly to go out at least two or three more times before leaving and go farther south to Cadogan and Talbot Inlet. We have also decided to try to leave a week earlier on the 25th rather than August 1st if Barry can manage it. There is little here at Alexandra to keep us longer except for my pond.

This morning was out at the reflecting pond painting at 8:30 AM. Painted three watercolours. Light continually changing. Can't work fast enough to put down what I want. Each painting always something of a disappointment insofar as it never measures up to my intentions or expectations. But perhaps in retrospect there may be some redeeming qualities. Took more photographs and a hike to second river to our east before it clouded over in afternoon to almost solid overcast. Walk more pleasant than in other direction. Not as much water and muskeg.

Talked to Jim, Barry's assistant, this evening on the skid to let him know we would like our return reservations changed to leave on the 25th, a week earlier since it is very limited here and not much more we can do. He said he would make the changes for us and put us down for a helicopter on Saturday the 18th. Also, it seems they are to drop other people off here tomorrow but it isn't clear where or how long they will be staying and what this will mean for the rest of our stay here. He will clarify in the morning.

These skids become very time-consuming particularly if you have any traffic. It can last over an hour and one listens to all manner of conversations ranging from instructions for operating equipment to orders for machinery parts to grocery lists and personal messages from all the many parties scattered across the Arctic and held together by these incredible little radios. The airplane as well

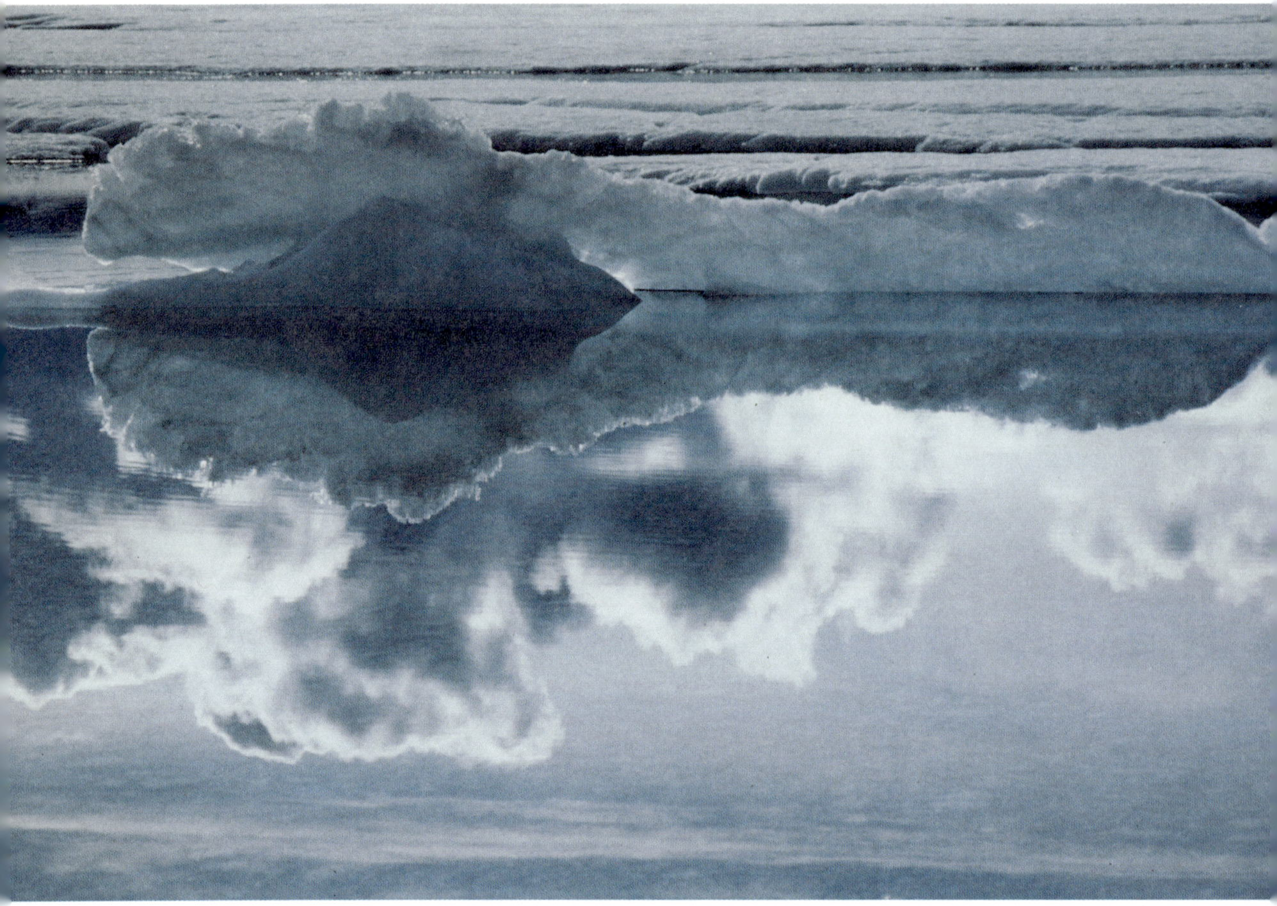

HANS DOMMASCH, **Ellesmere Island** | 1987

as the radio form the lifeline of the North. Like the sound of the human voice, the solitary drone of a distant approaching aircraft has profound significance in the silence of this remote land.

16.VII.87

THURSDAY

THIS MORNING WENT out to the pond at about 8 AM to snap some photographs. The sky clear, sun shining, light perfect, but a strong wind from the north that disturbed the surface of the pond sufficiently to eliminate reflections. Wait until wind subsides, some reflections return and I snap three photos that seem to catch something of what I'm after only to discover that the dark slide has not been removed from the camera. I keep forgetting this necessary procedure.

Return to pool to paint; wind is back. After a while it subsides and reflections return. Paint three studies in next three hours and get increasingly numb from the cold. At one point reaching for a brush I fall off my stool—whose bottom is too small and makes a precarious perch at best even with the piece of plywood I have placed under it. Later my paint box falls off its perch and everything is scattered on the rocks. This is what drives even the most dedicated of landscape painters into their studios! Yet it's never the same there. It becomes something different without the direct contact with nature. The Impressionists knew this as did Cézanne. Working in the studio one lacks or misses the physical or sensory stimulus and interaction with nature.

Yet art changes even with the source remaining the same. One could not conceive of the possibility of constructing a relief in the presence of nature. The process is too complex and involved. That is why watercolour serves as a direct, more immediate medium for making studies in response to what one sees. God knows, that is difficult enough, if not impossible!

Beyond obvious dimensional or spatial contrasts, there are great differences between painting a watercolour and constructing a relief. Where some of these watercolours can be done in an hour or two, a relief has often occupied me for several years or more. With watercolour nothing can be subtracted or removed once put down, while the relief can be added to, altered or subtracted from throughout the process of conception and realization. The relief, while appearing deceptively simple, is actually far more densely complex and involves an extended developmental process. Most of this process remains hidden or invisible in the final work whereas each watercolour is naked and transparent, revealing itself and its process completely.

Confronting my pool every morning, in which the mountains and glacier are reflected, has given me numerous ideas for new constructed reliefs. Some time ago, I began, but never completed, several reliefs in which reflecting and transparent materials were incorporated. I am anxious to get back to them to develop these new conceptions and see how or if I may overcome some of the problems I encountered in dealing for the first time with transparency and reflection in three-dimensional space.

After lunch, helicopter arrives dropping off two young scientists—Greg and Chris who are from Edmonton and will be staying here until Saturday. Shortly after, another landing with three or four other people who are part of Schledermann's party who will be staying overnight and taken out by Otter tomorrow back to Resolute. One of the group has keys for all the buildings so people will bunk in other places but they will likely use our kitchen facilities. (There goes the peace and quiet, the privacy, the Arctic silence we were taking for granted.) They all seem like very nice and interesting people—plant ecologists, geographers, archaeologists, geologists, etc. To be sure, our solitude—often difficult yet so necessary—shall be interrupted for the next few days.

Following coffee together, I go off with my camera as it is a sunny, bright afternoon. On my way back meet Greg and Chris who are on their way for a hike to the glacier. Greg says that the helicopter brought another load including a film crew from California doing a film on the Arctic for PBS (I begin to have visions of a world inhabited only by film crews who, after filming everything on earth, busily film each other). They will also be flying out tomorrow. Suddenly there are eight people here besides ourselves.

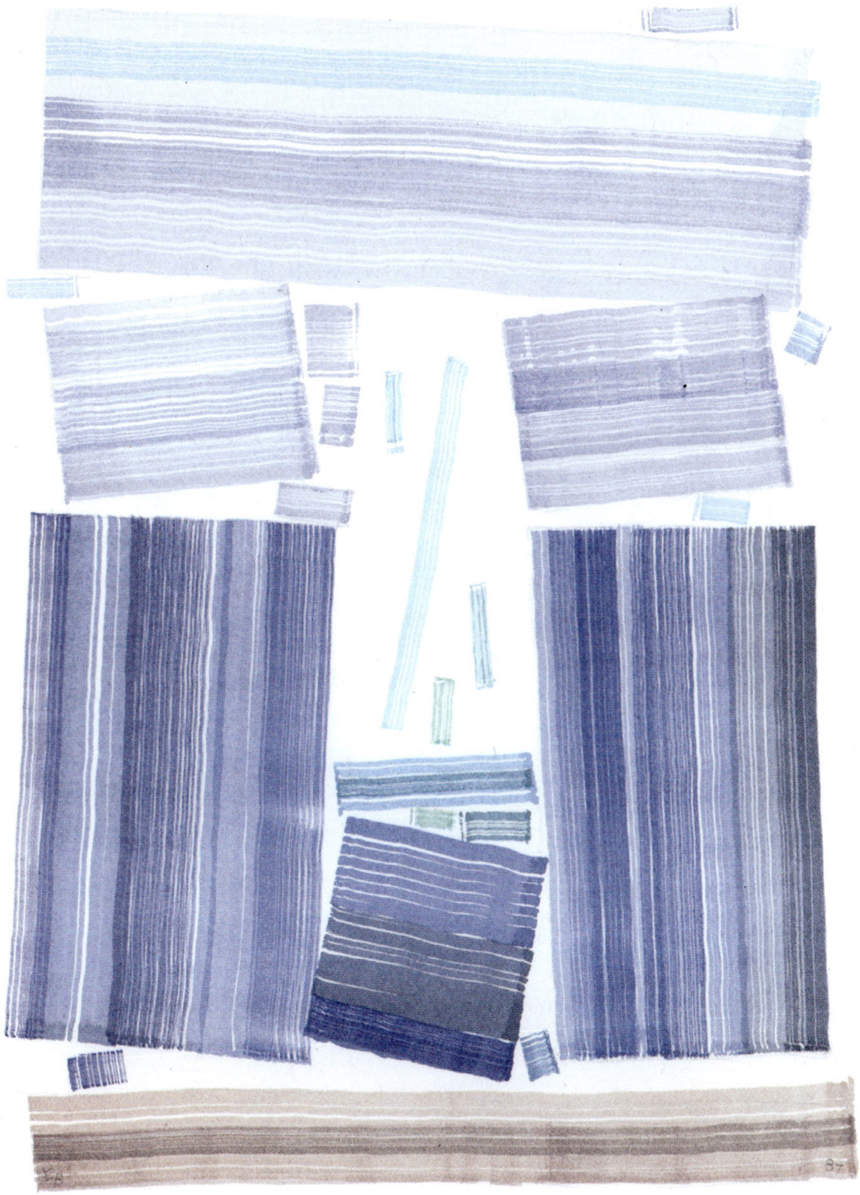

Arctic Study No. 42 | 1987 WATERCOLOUR ON PAPER, 33.6 × 27.3 CM

Vera, an oceanographer from Alaska up here studying polynyas (open, unfrozen waters appearing in the otherwise frozen Arctic seas), cooks dinner for all ten of us using stove in our house that has large table in kitchen and sufficient chairs. Menu: canned corned beef, freeze-dried peas, Kraft Dinner and applesauce. After dinner and much amusing talk, one more trip back to my reflecting pool around 10 PM with the sun in the northwest shining brightly in a clear sky. Reflections totally different—quite beautiful. I may stay up one night and try to do some studies around midnight.

My relatively small reflecting pond bears some comparison to Walden in that one could spend an entire year here, studying the unending changes, painting, thinking and learning much. But unlike Thoreau, I could not stand to be away from my wife and daughters and dog and live all by myself without dying of loneliness and a broken heart. Even sublime beauty could not entirely sustain me for such a long stretch of time away from Christina, Sarah, Thea and MacTavish, who of course would thoroughly love it here.

17.VII.87
FRIDAY

SIX OF THE PEOPLE were scheduled to leave on Twin Otter around 1 PM. Have breakfast with Greg and Gil, Vera's assistant, who lives in Fairbanks and went to Alaska from New York many years ago to escape civilization. He seems something of a misanthrope. Interesting to hear about the uncontrolled development of Fairbanks and how ugly it sounds circled by shopping malls. It would seem the mauling of America extends and grows insidiously—including Canada (which has probably outdone even the US in Edmonton) and Europe.

No painting this morning. Too much activity and too many distractions. Go for hike south of us to the mountain where Greg says there is an old fox den. Quite a climb to the den, a spectacular sight overlooking the valley and fjord below.

Otter finally arrives, but pilot and co-pilot haven't eaten and want some lunch. Finally around 2 PM the Otter takes off. Hans is at the den and Greg and

Chris are off for a day's hike. It's nice to have company but it's also nice when they leave so I can get back to my work, which is the reason I am here.

After a quiet lunch I go off to my reflecting pond with my paints. Mosquitoes are particularly bad so, much as I dislike it, must go back finally to put on repellent. Spend some time cleaning my paint boxes and palette and proceed with painting. Sometimes the first stroke can seem just right and start one off in a good direction.

Around 5:30 PM clean up and go back to house. Take the pail to get some water and go to the river for a wash.

About 6:30 PM a helicopter arrives with three RCMP officers, two army men and the pilot who appear at the doorway and all come into the house. A barrage of questions from the RCMP officer who is carrying a briefcase and camera. (I wonder if he has come to fingerprint me and take some mug shots.) They all walk around the place into our bedrooms and throughout the house. The soldiers ask if they can have some coffee, so I put on some water. They inspect all the buildings. It turns out they have heard about this place, which closed down in 1963, and just wanted to see the site. They flew over from Eureka. After a painful hour they finally leave. This place today has been like Grand Central Station. So much for Arctic isolation and loneliness.

Hans returns and we have supper. After meal take some more photographs till around 11 PM, then bed.

18.VII.87

SATURDAY

HELICOPTER SCHEDULED FOR our use today. On skid Barry says we can expect it around 10 AM and from previous conversation we understand it is very unlikely we will get helicopter again before we leave, so we want to make the most of it.

Helicopter arrives and the pilot is John, whom we met on Axel Heiberg. He is very amiable and gregarious, but very cautious about weight to be carried.

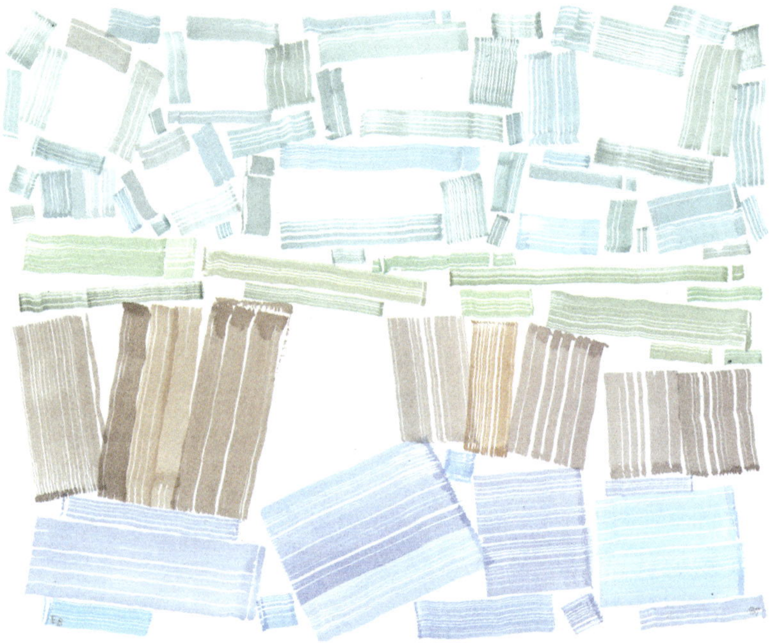

Arctic Study No. 27 | 1987 WATERCOLOUR ON RAG BOARD, 26.9 × 33.6 CM

(He weighs about 250 lbs.) As this will be a long trip he needs to carry a full tank of fuel to get us back. He shows me the six or so bolts that hold the motor to the cabin and that carry all the weight. As if this were not enough to put the fear of God into me about being overweight, he shows me the one nut that holds the large propeller to the drive shaft. They call it the "Jesus nut" because if it comes off it will bring you closer to Jesus. Hans and I, without further persuasion, strip down what we were planning to take and when we consider leaving half the food supply, John's caution seems to vanish; he thinks it an unnecessary sacrifice.

The helicopter loaded and refuelled, we take off for the day around 10:15 AM heading for Talbot Inlet and looking once again for icebergs.

The sea is beautiful. What is it about the blue of the ocean that brings such deep feeling of promise and joy, something definitely affirmative.

John talks almost continuously, pointing out endless details, and features we would not otherwise see. He shows us a mirage of what appears to be huge icebergs in the distance, but which are actually quite small. He points out Inuit longhouse remains and their ring houses all along the shore and on some of the islands we fly over.

We fly as far as Cape Faraday near Talbot Inlet but as it seems all frozen over with few icebergs, we circle back and set down on Cape Dunsterville, a rocky mountain, that seems to be sandstone and which overlooks a breathtaking expanse of deep blue ocean in which clean white icebergs are afloat. From this great height we can see Greenland, its mountains and glaciers some 50 miles away. We find a comfortable spot and have lunch.

The cape is a great spot for getting a feel of the open water of the ocean and its blue colour contrasts with the white icebergs, the clear blue sky and the reddish sandstone rock of the mountain. At the bottom of the rock is a kind of peach or pinkish orange colour that juts out in layers into the water. Spend an hour taking photographs. Don't for a moment consider painting, much as I would like to. For one thing I didn't think we'd have enough time, but more seriously, John followed us around and talked incessantly. Often interesting but too distracting for my concentration over a prolonged period of time.

We begin our return trip stopping along the way on another dramatic mountaintop, on a glacier with striking blue lakes of deep ultramarine to cerulean blue. Whenever we see an interesting iceberg, John very obligingly circles it for us and even drops down once on an ice floe and another time lands on a huge iceberg—larger than a football field and about 75 feet above the sea.

Finally, we stop at Wade Point again and take John down to see the stone houses on the beach. He knows something about them and the fact that the Greely Expedition of the 1870s or thereabouts had stopped here in their desperate return journey. Pieces of their boat, which had copper nails or rivets, could be seen. Also the old tins that were used to store food. Evidently, they moved north, unable to locate a food cache that was supposed to be somewhere in the vicinity, and out of an expedition of around 23, only seven, including Greely, survived.

The light is brilliant and the icebergs on the fjord have pristine reflections in a kind of teal blue water that looks more like glass or mirror.

We fly from Wade Point back to Alexandra circling Pim Island. Again John points out the remains of stone longhouses on which the Inuit placed the ribs of whales, like rafters, which would be covered by skins. Some are about 1,500 years old. Near one we fly over, there are the complete skeletons of two whales. As it happens, Peter Schledermann is camped with a small party on the island, so John puts the copter down near their camp. Peter comes down and John shows him the map. All the places we have seen are familiar to Peter.

Up again and back to Alexandra. It was an exciting day and exhausting. We saw too much and after a while one can't absorb anymore. The helicopter is of course a truly marvellous machine for seeing and covering miles of countryside. But there is a vast difference between flying over and being set down and walking. Flying, one soon loses a sense of scale and distance and gets an overview. It is by no means a substitute for walking where one gets direct experience of magnitudes and more sensory contact with the reality of the place. And finally, one only gets to know a place by staying there. The quick glance and overview is extremely valuable but cannot take the place of the prolonged intimate encounter.

Greg pointed out an Arctic fox that came quite close to our house. She was smaller than I expected—about the size of a medium-sized cat, but very frail looking. Much smaller than our coyotes at home. Yet Greg assures me they attack an Arctic hare without difficulty.

19.VII.87
SUNDAY

TALKED TO BARRY after skid and it is now confirmed we will stay on here until Wednesday, Thursday or Friday when we will be picked up by the Otter and taken back to Resolute. Our reservations have been confirmed for Saturday, July 25. Greg and Chris will be picked up this afternoon or tomorrow.

Hans and I are pleased that we will have some more time here by ourselves to wind down and savour the closing days of our Arctic journey. I am pleased that it will give me some more engagements with my watercolours and the reflecting pond.

After breakfast went out to paint and finished one. The struggle with the mosquitoes was fierce. Foolishly I came out without putting repellent on. But I wouldn't battle them further to make a second painting. I have been making pencil sketches and notes and hopefully with some of the colour transparencies I have taken I can paint some more at home in my studio while the experience is still fresh.

Today very warm. And of course the warmer it is the more active the mosquitoes.

In afternoon I took walk back to the river. Decided not to lug camera and tripod, etc., and of course saw numerous things I will have to come back to photograph, among them some lovely purply flowers appropriately called River Beauty.

Hans more practical and industrious. Took a bath in one of our ponds nearby and washed his clothes. He puts me to shame as I idle away the warm afternoon in the sun.

Around 6 PM we hear thunderous noise in the sky and an enormous army helicopter sets down. We are again visited by the RCMP. The same questions: who we are, our names, etc. This officer visits all the buildings taking video pictures. He explains that he knew some of the original officers who served here in this legendary post and is concerned about its safekeeping. Pilot says his Chinook is the largest helicopter in Canadian army and has back door into which a truck could be driven. Finally, as they make ready to depart the two large propellers cause a terrific wind with sand flying in all directions. I am glad to see it leave and take with it the dreadful noise it makes. How many more visits will we have from the RCMP before we leave we wonder.

20.VII.87

MONDAY

TODAY GREG AND CHRIS are scheduled to leave, probably later this afternoon. After the skid, learned that Barry Lopez, author of *Arctic Dreams*, will be dropped off here and spend two or three days awaiting a helicopter to take him to see Peter Schledermann. It is an amazing coincidence because the one book I brought up with me to read is *Arctic Dreams*. I only glanced at it but it was enough to realize that I liked the way he wrote very much, and because I am keeping this journal as a continuation of last year's, I decided not to read his book here. I wanted to respond directly to the Arctic and not be too influenced by the impressions of anyone else. In fact, from the little snippets I read, I suspect that if I read the book while here I could well cease writing in my journal. So, I decided to postpone the pleasure of reading it until after I return home. Life indeed works in curious ways, for now I have the pleasure of meeting the author before reading his book.

This morning went back to nature's mirror to gaze again at the reflections of sky, glacier and mountains and try my hand again at painting a construction of colour planes—my Arctic études or impromptus. Painted for almost three hours. Finished two studies, and around noon the Twin Otter arrived and touched down. As I began to gather up my painting things, I waved goodbye to Greg and Chris who departed.

When I got back met Barry Lopez to whom Hans was already talking. Barry joined us for lunch and it was a real pleasure to talk with him. He seemed very intelligent and sensitive and we had some good conversation.

Notably, I have tended to resent intrusions of which we have had far too many. This was a notable exception.

In the afternoon walked back to the river to photograph those things I saw yesterday afternoon without my camera. The light bright and warm. The river deeper and more turbulent as warm weather makes glacier melt more quickly. Snapped entire roll while walking along and standing in the river.

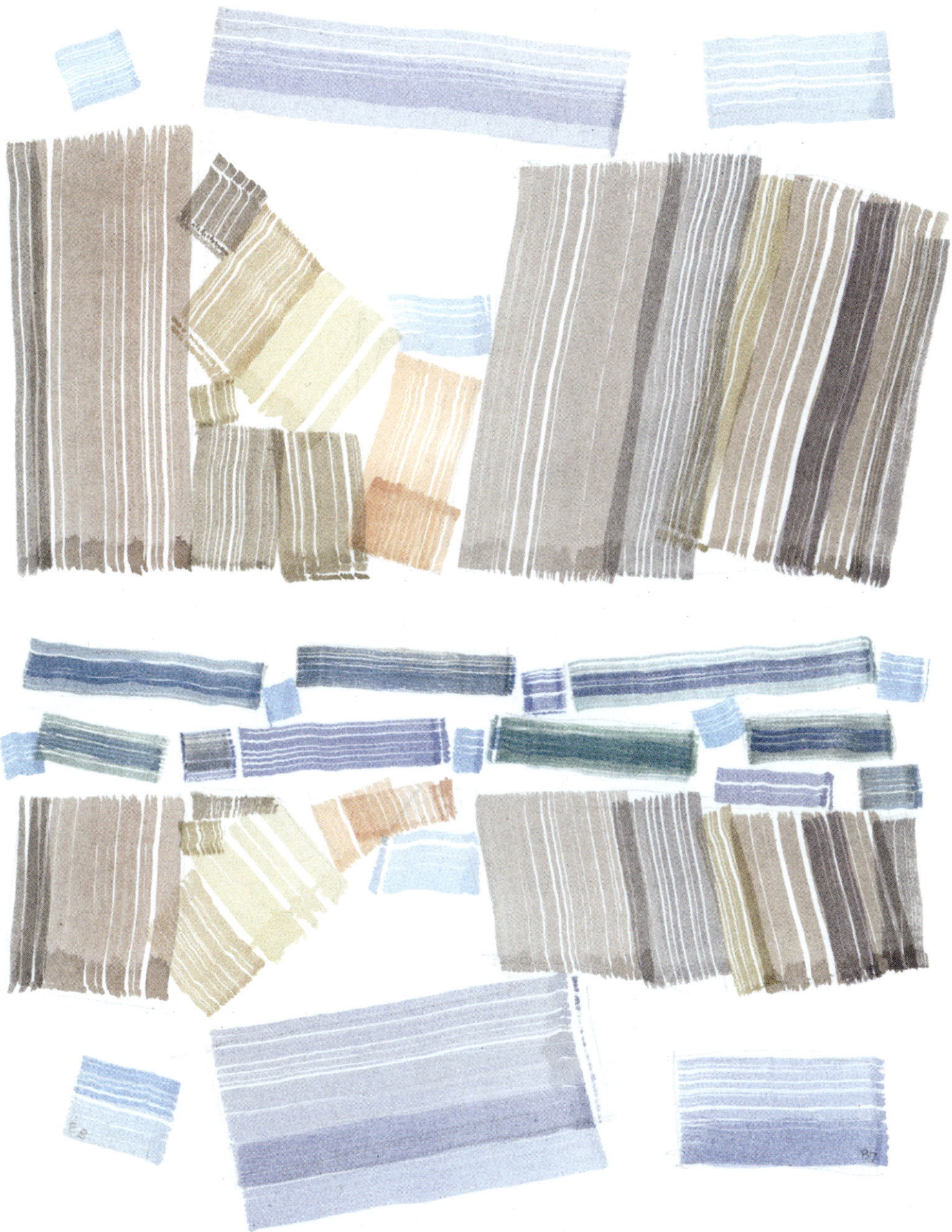

Arctic Study No. 29 | 1987
WATERCOLOUR ON MAT BOARD, 33.6 × 26.9 CM

Returned to house and shortly thereafter both Hans and then Barry returned from their respective hikes. We walked back to river to have a wash and get more drinking water.

After the skid, made supper—beans, bacon, corn and tomatoes. More interesting conversation about the artist or writer. Barry tells us of the success of his book and that it is now being translated into numerous languages and published in various countries. Talk of the problems of coping with success and his wish to return to anonymity.

The light is golden tonight at 10 PM. Hans decides to stay up all night taking photographs in this unique Arctic evening light before leaving.

The light coupled with the peacefulness makes this time supremely idyllic. Surrounded by ice and glacier there is nevertheless a warmth here—emanations of Elysium.

I noticed this evening that the level of my pond has dropped five or six inches since we first arrived. Also, I notice steam rising from its surface, the water being heated by the sun is warmer than the air and evaporation is taking place. In another week's time there may be no more pool.

And what of all the reflections I have seen and photographed and painted? They too will have vanished into the air, without a trace. There is no doubt the reflections were as real as the mountains and glaciers themselves and part of all those natural processes of formation or creation and destruction. Like our very lives—our mortalities that are and then are not—the reflections have been, as has the pond and as I have, and then will be no more.

21.VII.87
TUESDAY

VERY RESTLESS NIGHT of broken sleep, which can't be blamed on Hans who stayed up till 3 AM taking photographs and very thoughtfully had moved his sleeping bag to another room of the building so he wouldn't disturb me. Have I become so used to Hans' snoring that the silence kept me awake?

After skid and breakfast have more interesting conversation with Barry Lopez about the state of the world and in particular some of the depressing things happening in the USA.

Returned to my pond and painted one watercolour. Once I start painting the morning vanishes before I know. I usually end feeling I've somewhat missed the mark of my aim or intention. Sometimes closer, sometimes further, but never dead on. There's always the next one, the next try.

Lunch and then a little sleep. Somewhat revived by the short nap but still remain tired. Take my afternoon hike to the river and beyond on what is another clear and sun-warmed day. The difference between being in the sun and the shade is at least 10 degrees Celsius or more.

During walk the silence and peace is once again shattered by the appearance of the same enormous army helicopter that lands. I am thankful that I am so far away.

Somehow if I ever return to the Arctic again, I would not particularly want to come back to Alexandra. Despite the very attractive comforts and convenience of the place, it is far too busy for my taste. There are disruptions enough at home, one hardly needs them here. At Otto Fjord last year we lived in our tents, were often cold, but there were no intrusions of any kind.

When I got back, the helicopter was just taking off. Hans informed me that the pilot agreed to take Barry over to Peter Schledermann's camp if he can land nearby, so Barry was already on the plane. We had visions of the helicopter blowing all Schledermann's tents apart if he landed too close.

Up went the monster and Barry was sitting in the back waving to us as they took off. Ten minutes later the helicopter returned overhead on its way back to Eureka, so I guess Barry landed okay.

Sorry to see him leave as he was such an interesting person to talk to. But that is typical here in the Arctic where one never knows what will happen next as plans continually change. He left me his name and address and asked me to send him a copy of *The Structurist*. While I shall miss the opportunity of talking further to this fine American writer, I must admit that I welcome the chance to spend our last few days here without company. For where art is concerned there cannot be too much concentration and everything else, however enjoyable and of value, becomes a distraction. Let us hope that the next few days will not bring further visitors, particularly from the RCMP or the Canadian army.

22.VII.87
WEDNESDAY

ANOTHER RESTLESS NIGHT even though I was so exhausted I went to bed at 9:30 PM.

One of the things that Greg did when he arrived was to reinstate the toilet that was on its side. With no one here before then we merely used our little shovel leaving neat little circles on the tundra of potentially well-fertilized soil. The toilet became of course another luxury. About two blocks away it faces out on the bay so one sits and looks out on a magnificent view every morning. We call it the White House and frequently say we are going to pay our respects to Ronald Reagan or just Ronnie.

Painted at the pond for four hours, did two watercolours. Mosquitoes had mercy on me and work went fairly well. As we are now flying home from Resolute on the 25th, we expect to have the Otter take us out of here either tomorrow or Friday. Much packing to be done. Should learn this evening on the skid when they will come for us.

The prospect of a hot shower and washing my hair after three weeks is wonderful. The expectation of seeing Christina again and the girls and the pup are beyond belief, it seems that I've been away so long. The anticipation of leaving this blissful land and confronting civilization again makes me nervous and uneasy. As last time, I expect there to be considerable shock and adjustment.

After lunch, which Hans had already made when I got back at about 1 PM, had a short nap. Then decided to try crossing the rivers to the east of us since we learned that the cabin next door had pairs of hip-waders. The tide was out so we walked close to the shore, but the second river proved too deep and fast for us since we didn't want to risk getting our cameras wet. Nevertheless, the walk in the sun over the melting snow was a delight and we could wade out to some of the grounded bergs.

Back to the river for drinking water and a wash. Each evening we return the river is higher and faster. The water is no longer crystal clear as it was when we first came. Now it is filled with sand and needs to stand awhile for the sediment to settle.

We notice too, increasingly, the silence is often broken with a loud crash. Pieces of icebergs are breaking off and falling into the water.

One of the things I observed about my little studies from the reflecting pond is that the colour planes have a tension and movement about them, a balance and counter-balance, a dynamic symmetry that parallels, quite unconsciously, something of the tensions and forces, the manifestations of which are seen all around here. The diastrophic forming of the mountains themselves, the movement of the glaciers, and of the rocks and earth by them, the force of the rushing melting water, and the power of its freezing and thawing are all processes of the morphology of the earth and the geological landscape. Something of that elemental tension and complementary opposition of forces is also in the studies where the opposition is between the colours, their relative size and positions in the limited space. All these forces seek at the same time a coordination toward some dynamic equilibrium—if one is lucky. That kind of parallel is in a sense an analogue or metaphor of processes between art and nature, albeit in an abstract and minute magnitude where the art is concerned. There is a geology of art that I am increasingly conscious of.

On the skid we are told we will be picked up by the Otter tomorrow sometime. We both regret leaving this place.

Every night when I get up to pee two or three times, I am always amazed at the quality of the midnight sun—golden light that is warm and soft. Our 21 days in the Arctic have been one continuous day, a great feast of light. I wonder as I see the birds at all hours, when do they or the other animals sleep?

23.VII.87

THURSDAY

WE ARE TO RADIO BACK at 2 PM for confirmation of time we will be picked up.

At 8 AM one last go at the reflecting pool. Work until 11:30 AM and finish one larger size and three smaller colour studies. Then I must begin to pack and clean up the place.

Plane scheduled to pick us up at about 3:30 PM. Day is beautiful. Much more ice melted in the bay and water a magnificent blue green I've never seen here before. One regret is not seeing all the ice out around the first week of August, and all the change of colours I will not see. It is not so much the site here with its buildings and other features, but this Arctic land/sea/light/space ever-changing and unfolding before one's eyes, ever nascent.

Twin Otter arrived around 3:30 PM. We load up plane and by 4 PM we are airborne heading south to Grise Fiord on the southeast tip of Ellesmere to refuel. Scenery from the plane breathtaking as we fly over surrounding glaciers, mountains and fjords and eventually through and above magnificent clouds. About 6 PM we descend toward Grise (this is the place where an Inuit community was moved in order to establish Arctic sovereignty); it seems like a rather grim assortment of buildings. Because of turbulence we do not land and proceed on to Truelove on Devon Island. This settlement is on very low land where we discover upon landing a large community of young people doing research. This is an established base of the Arctic Institute and we learn many of the young men and women are graduate students. The buildings are relatively substantial and they seem to have many of the amenities an ordinary tent camp would never have. We meet Greg and Chris who are heading back to Resolute and on to Polar Bear Pass.

After refuelling we are airborne with three additional passengers and considerably more luggage so that we must all climb over a mountain of gear to get to seats at the front.

On our return flight to Resolute, after flying for almost an hour across Devon, the pilot tells us to fasten seat belts, we will be landing again. He circles a barren rocky bluff along the coast that rises about 1,000 feet above the sea. We note a white form running in the opposite direction from the approaching plane. It is a solitary polar bear on this plateau high above the shore. When the plane circles back, the bear runs in the opposite direction. About a mile away we note the solitary figure of a man waiting for the plane to pick him up. We learn later that neither he nor the pilot were aware of the bear. I was struck by the two solitary creatures on this high plateau oblivious of each other's existence. The one prowling the vast land in search of food, the other, an elderly man, a botanist, who had camped out here for several weeks by himself, in search of Arctic plant life. One was the supreme king of the Arctic realm. The other, frail by comparison, embodying the uniquely indomitable human spirit. The determination and courage of this man, living on this windswept coast in isolation, was admirable. The plane made an impressive landing on the sharp rocks, picked up our new passenger and his gear and took off for our last leg to Resolute.

Landed in Resolute around 9 PM quite exhausted and hungry. The place was overcrowded with people waiting to go south. We were taken back to Bob's trailer to sleep again after some food that was waiting for us in the dining room.

24.VII.87
FRIDAY

VERY RESTLESS NIGHT; six people are sleeping in the trailer and Hans outdoing himself in volume and pitch with his snoring. After breakfast walked to air terminal where we were told we could find ticket agent at 9 AM to change and confirm our tickets. Waited for 40 minutes and then tried to use pay phone to find out when the ticket agent really would be there.

After numerous calls, which included several Zenith numbers for long distance to Montreal and Toronto, and considerable confusion, finally got the cargo agent here, who happened also to be ticket agent. Was told that he opens at 1 PM to passengers. This seems typical of Resolute, where one is constantly waiting in uncertainty as to one's further movements, one's destiny. Like Kafka's

[Josef] K., one is aware of a nameless or invisible bureaucratic hierarchy at work with which one can have no direct simple communication. This is the worst aspect of the North, the interminable waiting. Hans calls Resolute the asshole of the North. I've heard that description used for Churchill and several other places. He hastens to add that this is an important part of the anatomy.

Our tickets, after some hassles, have now changed and confirmed as far as Edmonton and we are scheduled to leave at 4:30 PM tomorrow. So, we are slowly being drawn into the orbit of civilization. The debriefing, as the army calls transitions from one realm to another—from outer space back to planet Earth—begins here in Resolute as the Arctic experience must be terminated.

25.VII.87
SATURDAY

TODAY IS THE DAY of our departure, a day anticipated with eagerness to leave Resolute and get back to my home and loved ones. Yet also a day of regret at leaving behind the pristine light and beauty of Ellesmere, the peace, the space, the skies, glaciers, mountains, fjords, sea and icebergs and the overwhelming experience of living close to all that for three weeks. There is also anxiety about the shock of civilization again and adjusting to it and reluctantly, but inevitably, giving up the Arctic, which has gradually occupied one's whole being with its radiance, driving out all other mundane or trivial considerations or preoccupations.

With a good part of day ahead of us before departure, we manage to check our baggage after breakfast and get the use of the jeep for the morning. We drive out to Inuit village where we were yesterday and previously when we first arrived. Yesterday we visited an Inuit carver. I asked him if he had two small pieces I could buy for my daughters. He said he didn't, but to come back tomorrow. I had visions of his working feverishly all night. Someone else saw him last evening on his way to go fishing. So, when we visited him again I didn't expect anything. To my surprise, he said he had some small pieces in his house. Disappeared and emerged with four different pieces. The two I selected were of a duck or bird and a polar bear. The bird looked somewhat incomplete but in a pleasing sort of way. I asked if it was finished. He replied, shrugging his shoulders, it needed a little more finishing or polishing. When I asked if he was going to finish it, he again shrugged with an emphatic "no." There was no questioning that for him it was finished in its unfinished state. He had a marvellous face and agreed to sign the pieces, while Hans photographed him. There was a quiet dignity about this man.

After a hearty lunch of Arctic char, our last meal here, we eventually made our way to the air terminal. A crowd began to gather for arrivals and departures before the 737 landed. It was a long wait before we eventually left since there was some damage to the hydraulic support on the front wheel. Somehow the crowd of people was exhausting, as the flight was delayed over an hour.

For three weeks I had not read a newspaper, looked at television or listened to the radio outside of our daily skid. I hadn't really missed any of it and was not quite ready to re-engage my senses and consciousness with the electronic and commercial communication media. Somehow the daily news seemed of little interest or consequence.

Normally at home I listen a great deal to classical music on FM radio or on phonograph both in my studio and house as well as the FM radio in the car. Music is an important part of my daily life. Here somehow, I do not miss it at all, which surprises me. Could it be that the space and ever-changing light amidst the profound silence here in this vast landscape make other kinds of human music seem trivial or unnecessary? The Arctic seems to minimize almost everything we hold dear and vital back home by comparison. I recall that when I returned from the North last time only gradually could I begin to listen to music again without it being a distraction or intrusion or something I must give my total attention. Perhaps many of us use music in our daily lives as a kind of protective shroud or cocoon to shelter us from the noise and other sensory assaults that urban living constantly makes upon us. Is this not a kind of abuse or misuse of music? Are we increasingly neglecting all our arts by half-listening, half-looking?

Now I am on an airplane heading for Edmonton with inane muzak blaring. The floodgates of civilization or culture are being thrown wide open and I'm swamped by it all. Where are those Arctic spaces in which I felt so free?

In the high Arctic one can still travel for many hundreds of miles in all directions without any sign of humanity. Inevitably and increasingly of course there are the ubiquitous steel fuel drums painted red or yellow or simply rusting. (Hans compared humankind's leaving of fuel drums to the wolf who urinates to mark out his territory.) But these are relatively few and far between given the vast spaces and difficult terrain. When one moves south and finally to the most concentrated centres of human habitation, the city, humankind's presence is everywhere. There is hardly anything left that has not, in some way, been altered, moved, tampered with, controlled, befouled or polluted. The aggressive hand of humans and our machines are more often than not unpleasant intrusions and devoid of concern or harmony with nature. Much of it is ugly, but we adapt to it and become blind to its harsh and sleazy character. (Unlike the wolf's urine, much of what we leave behind is not biodegradable and often has long-range destructive consequences.)

So, once again, I have come down from Arcadia and wonder: What will become of it? How can the North be protected and used wisely for our own future preservation? Inevitably, living in the high Arctic raises questions of both personal and social kinds. It asks of one: Who am I? What am I? How can I return and live my life in a manner that reflects what I have learned and loved in the North? For, if nothing else, the Arctic experience peels the protective layers from our eyes and makes us see the raw ugliness of our society, the crass materialism, the false values we embrace. (This includes much contemporary art, which merely reflect these same values.) It does this in a stunning manner with all the severity of culture shock. Returning to what we left behind, we suddenly see the mess we have made and wonder why. Are cars, television, advertising and all the goodies and temptations of modern living really that important and worth the price they exact from our essential well-being?

One resists in vain these comforts and seductions, despite the awareness that we have lost something of profound importance in the process. The ancient wisdom of the Inuit culture, like that of other Indigenous North Americans, now fast disappearing if not already lost forever, is victim of the wholesale propagation of our way of life. This loss is unfathomable.

We know some of the ills and delusions of our culture—at least there is some measure of agreement among our finest critics—but we are not sure about how to cure them, what we should do. Where are the cultural therapists that can treat what increasingly ails us? We have physio-, psycho-, occupational and other therapies, but we have not developed any cultural therapies that have the wisdom and the power to effect the needed transformations that can stop the self-consuming, self-destroying directions that prevail.

It occurs to me that the high Arctic is the ultimate remaining watershed for civilization as a retreat for broad reflection, speculation, contemplation or meditation on questions of the human condition. From this ancient, relatively unspoiled site crowning our planet, we can find the perspective needed to consider what we have wrought on this earth, and wherein lies our salvation.

Only such profound space, silence and radiant light as are still found in the Arctic can yet provide the objectivity for such deliberations on our future. Could it not be made to serve the world as a place where our leaders and directors, our presidents and chairmen of nations and multinational corporations would be required to visit and stay in a simple tent periodically? Surely an immodest proposal. Impracticable, to say the least. (Can one imagine Reagan or Gorbachev living simply and solitarily in a tent for several weeks unconnected or unsurrounded by all the media, aides, advisors and secret service men?) Yet it is not impossible, given the will, for those of conviction and in search of new vision.

If it is not already too late, the high Arctic could conceivably become the world's Walden Pond—a last remnant of this planet that could be protected and remain undisturbed by man, inviolate, as the place from which a sane view of ourselves, and the world we have made and are making, is still possible.

Such a viewpoint could provide the possibilities, however difficult they may be, of finding new beginnings, alternative directions and some viable withdrawals from our worst forms of global madness and suicide. Ellesmere Island, and indeed much of the high Arctic, where the most ancient history of the earth itself is so visible, inspires reverence and humility. As such, it may well be the last genuine resource of our renewal.

26.VII.87
SUNDAY

SUCH WERE THE RUMINATIONS that consumed my mind most of the night as I lay awake in the king-sized bed in my large air-conditioned motel room. The hot shower in the morning was of course a welcome pleasure, yet I would not exchange it for our fresh cold river at Alexandra.

This early Sunday morning as I walked around the motel situated near the Edmonton airport, I was struck by the noise and ugliness of this man-made wasteland where everything seemed given over to commerce and advertising, the automobile and to gross hedonism. Where was there nourishment for the ear and the eye, for the spirit or the soul?

As we awaited our afternoon flight back to Saskatoon, we had brunch in the motel dining room and I continued to ponder the incredible contrast between the life we led for the past three weeks and the one we were fast returning to.

Life in the North seems simple by comparison to that at home. In our urban environment life becomes much more complex and one's time and attention are continually fractured and dispersed in many directions. Singular concentration and pursuit become a daily struggle. One learns to live without many things in the North and they are not really missed. Here the chain of complex "needs" and "dependencies" quickly encircle and persistently restrain. The temptations and distractions are endless and one is constantly trying to resist them. To keep one's life simple becomes a Herculean task.

One seeks clarity in art, as well as life. All artists, worthy of the name, pursue clarity of vision, clarity of purpose. Clarity rather than obfuscation. In our modern world one is befuddled and beguiled by the unrelenting pressures of

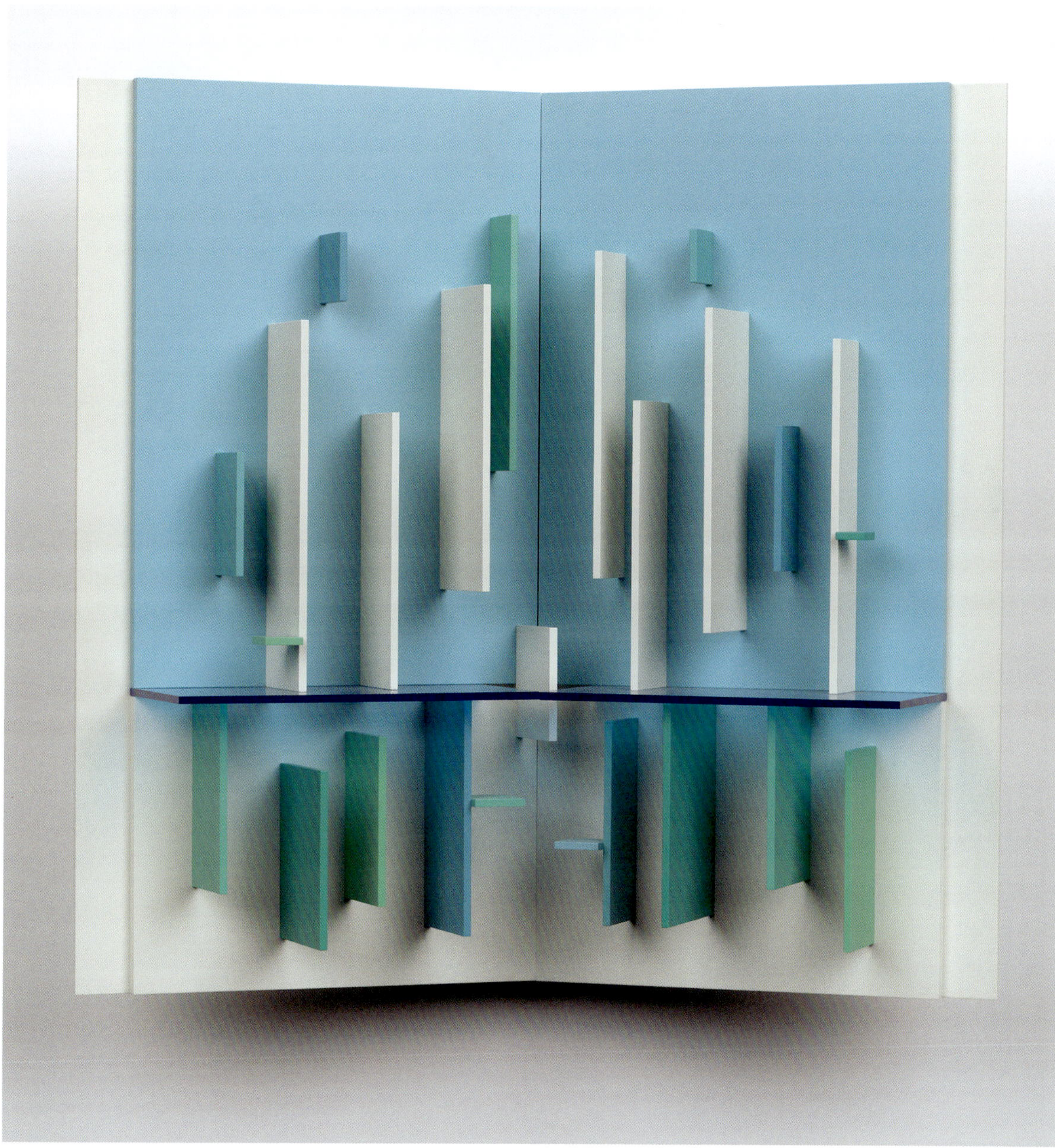

Multiplane Structurist Relief IV, No. 1 (Arctic Series) | 1986–1987
ENAMEL ON ALUMINUM AND PLEXIGLAS, 38.1 × 38.2 × 8.2 CM BEAVERBROOK ART GALLERY COLLECTION: GIFT OF ELI BORNSTEIN

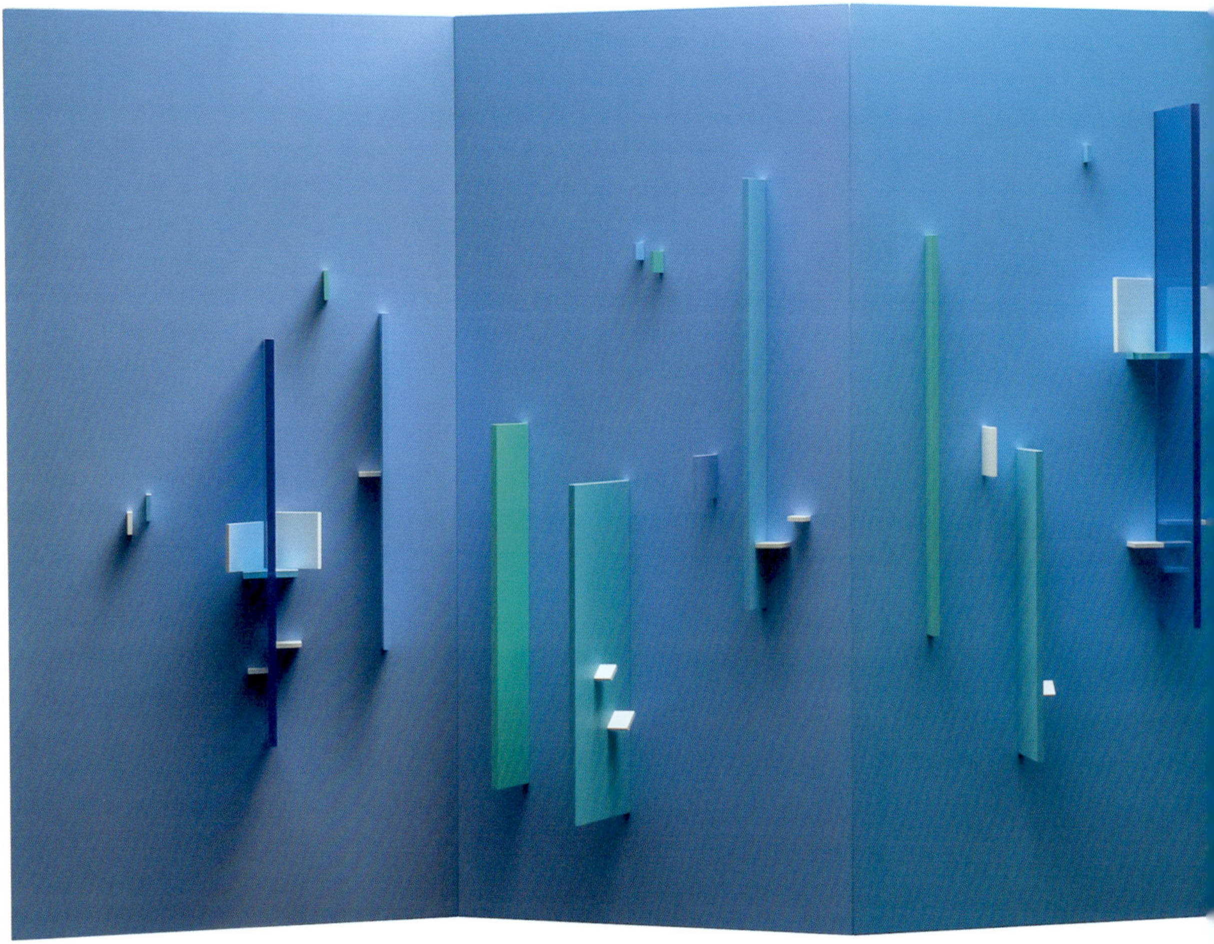

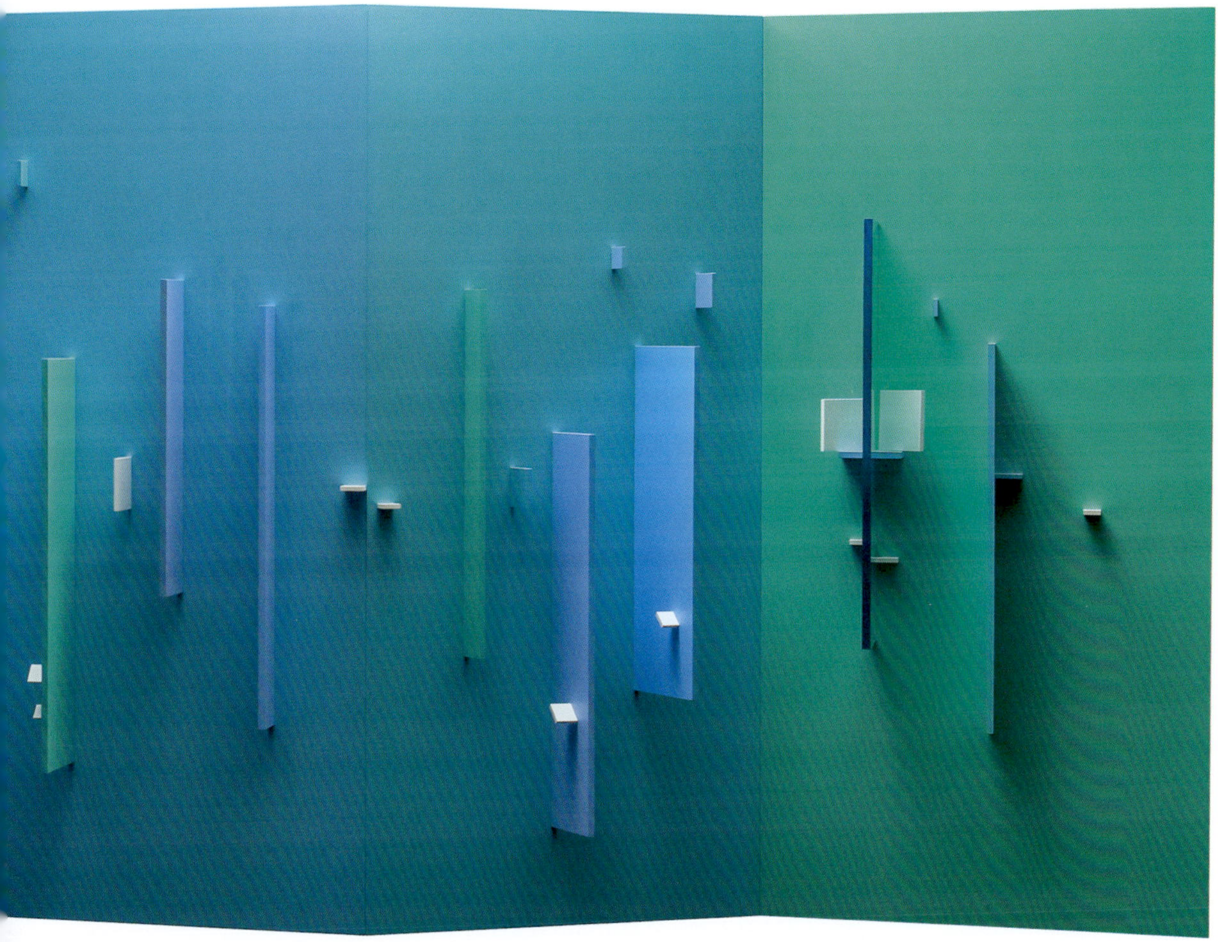

Hexaplane Structurist Relief No. 2 (Arctic Series) | 1995–1998

HOMAGE TO MURRAY ADASKIN. ACRYLIC ENAMEL ON ALUMINUM AND PLEXIGLAS, 67.2 × 182.2 × 15.9 CM

UNIVERSITY OF SASKATCHEWAN ART COLLECTION: GIFT OF DOROTHEA ADASKIN | PHOTOGRAPH BY TROY MAMER

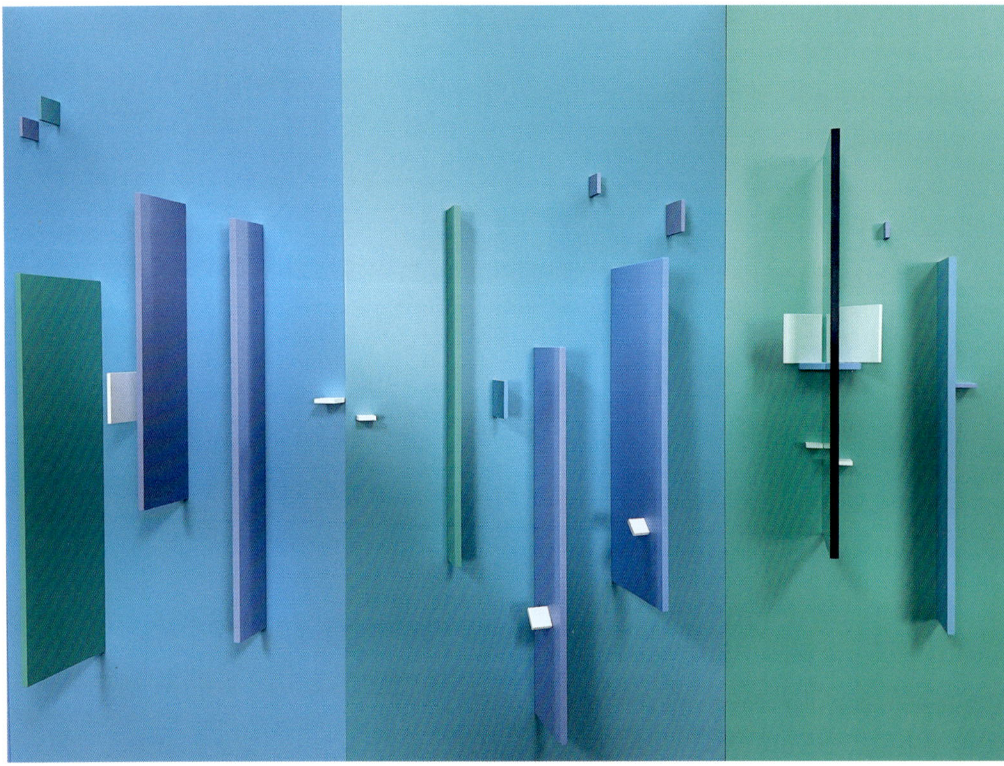

Hexaplane Structurist Relief No. 2 (Arctic Series), ***detail*** | 1995–1998
HOMAGE TO MURRAY ADASKIN. ACRYLIC ENAMEL ON ALUMINUM AND PLEXIGLAS, 67.2 × 182.2 × 15.9 CM
UNIVERSITY OF SASKATCHEWAN ART COLLECTION: GIFT OF DOROTHEA ADASKIN | PHOTOGRAPH BY DAVID BINDLE

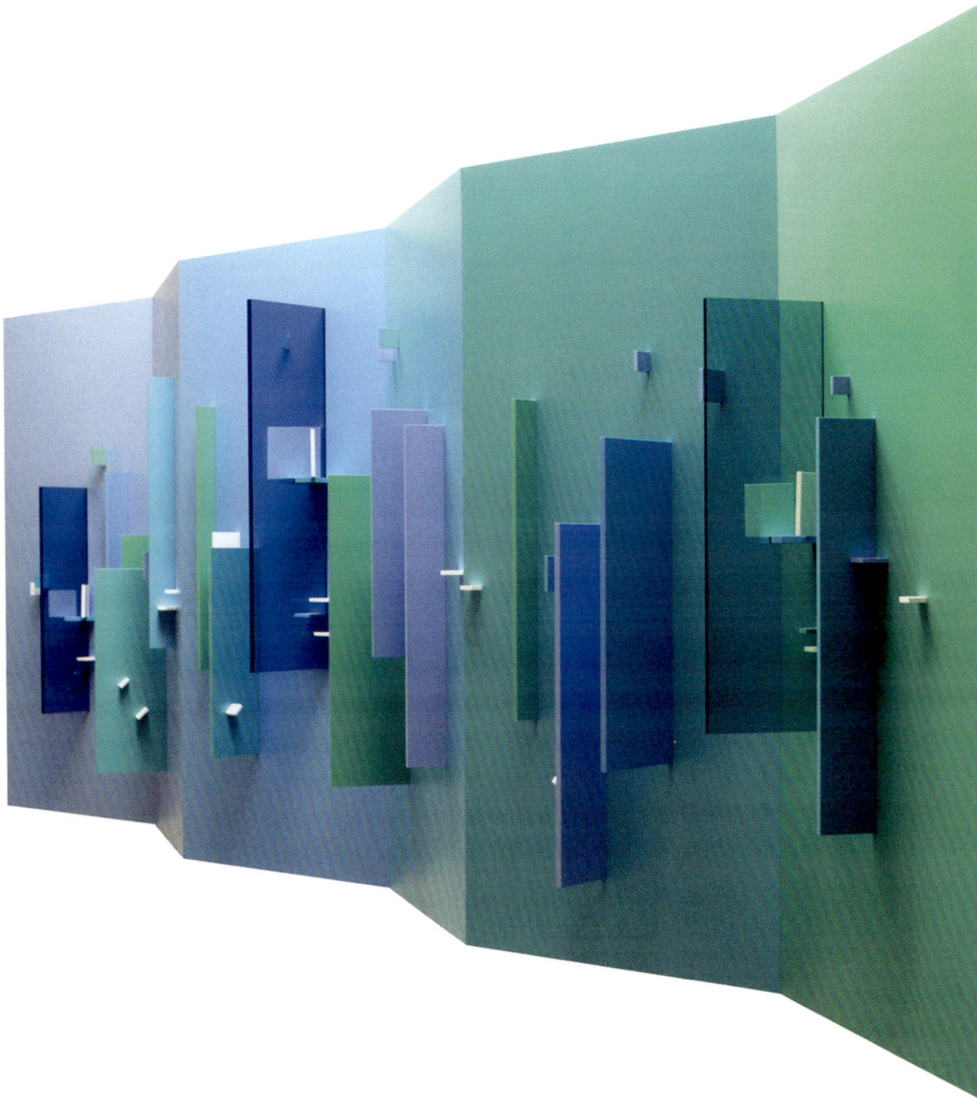

Hexaplane Structurist Relief No. 2 (Arctic Series) | 1995–1998
HOMAGE TO MURRAY ADASKIN. ACRYLIC ENAMEL ON ALUMINUM AND PLEXIGLAS, 67.2 × 182.2 × 15.9 CM
UNIVERSITY OF SASKATCHEWAN ART COLLECTION: GIFT OF DOROTHEA ADASKIN | PHOTOGRAPH BY TROY MAMER

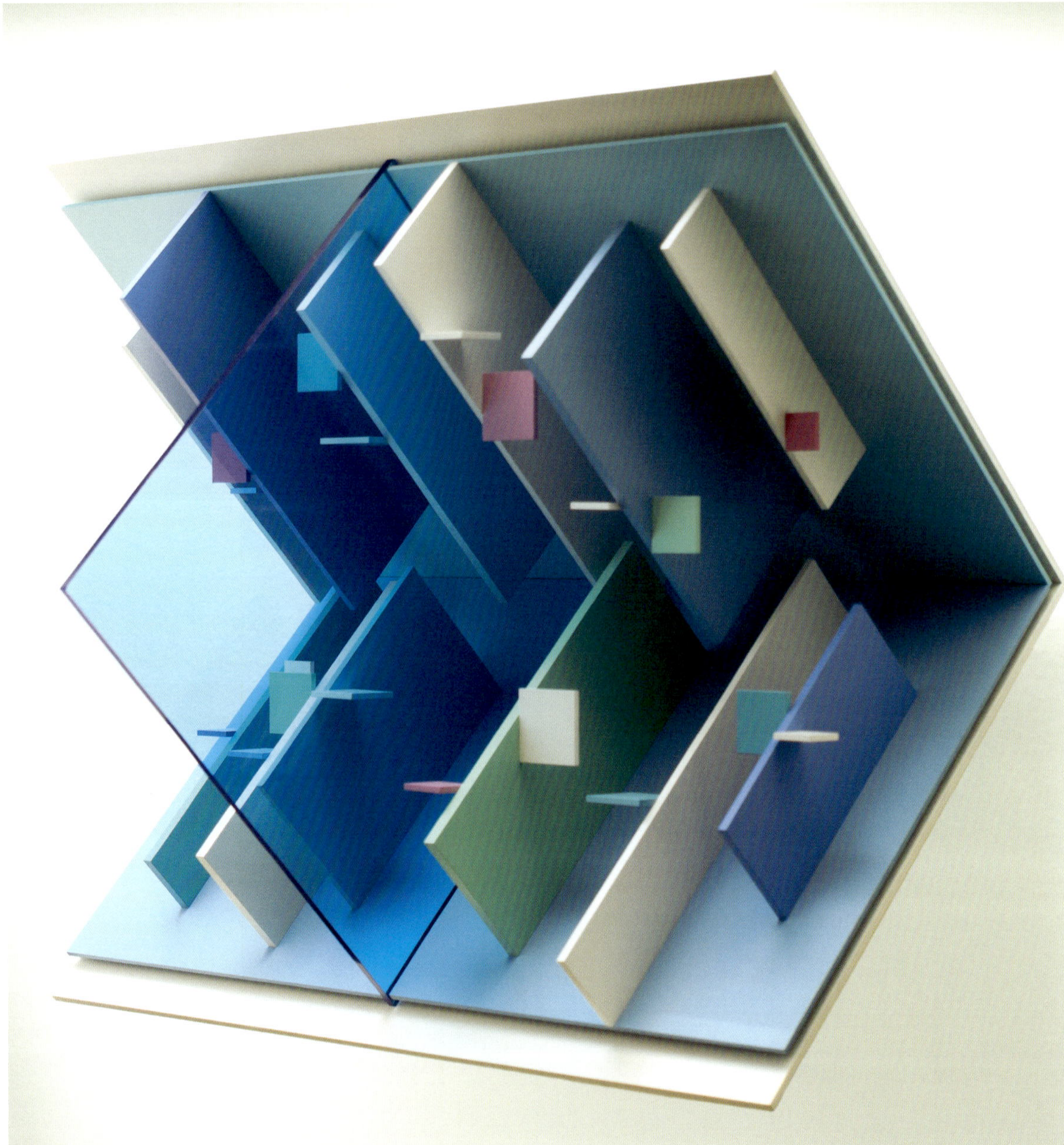

Double Plane Structurist Relief No. 18 (Arctic Series) | 1990–1992
ENAMEL ON PLEXIGLAS AND ALUMINUM, 39.4 × 43.2 × 39.8 CM PHOTOGRAPH BY TROY MAMER

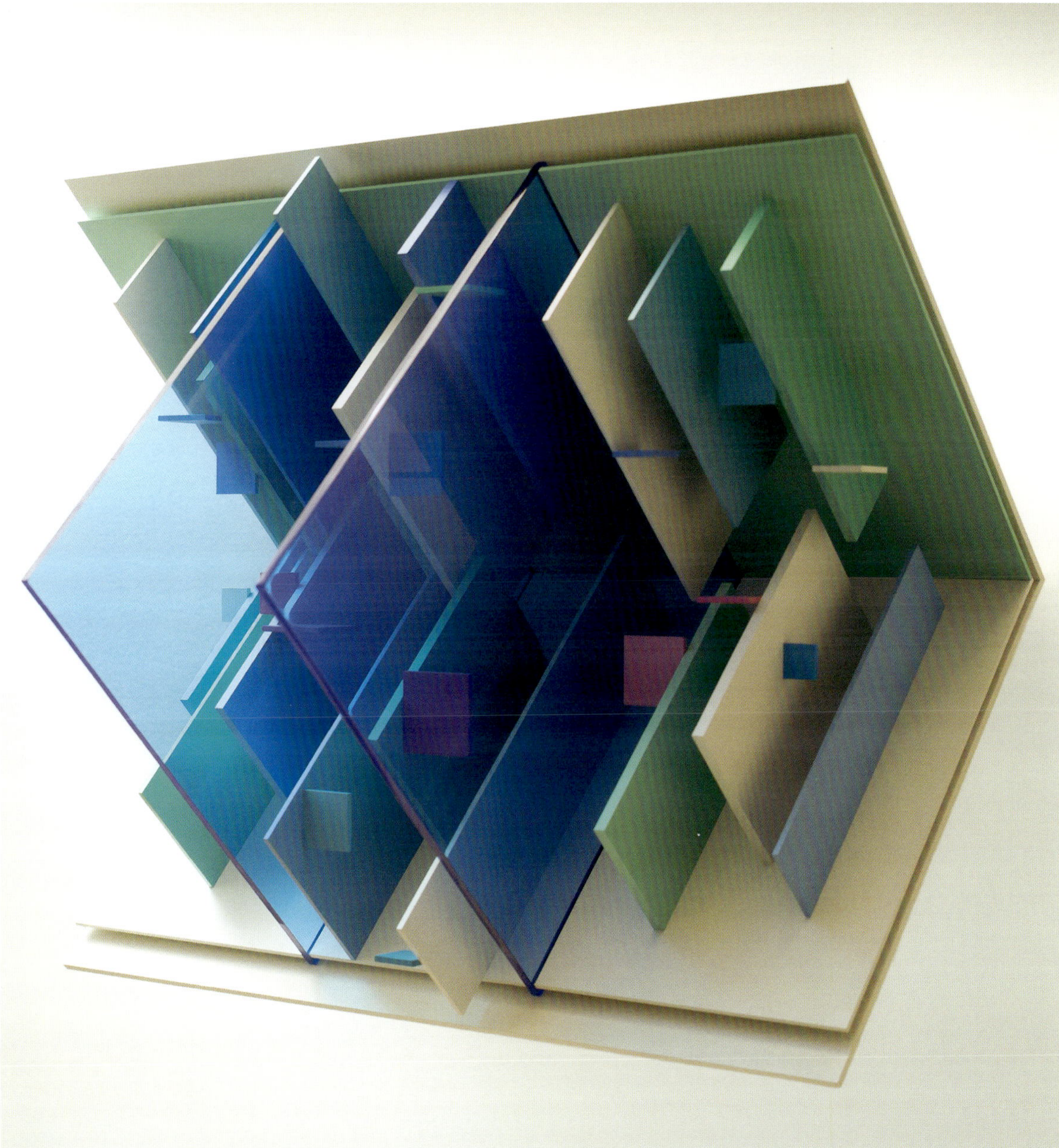

Double Plane Structurist Relief No. 20 (Arctic Series) | 1991–1992
ENAMEL ON PLEXIGLAS AND ALUMINUM, 49.2 × 53.3 × 47.9 CM PHOTOGRAPH BY TROY MAMER

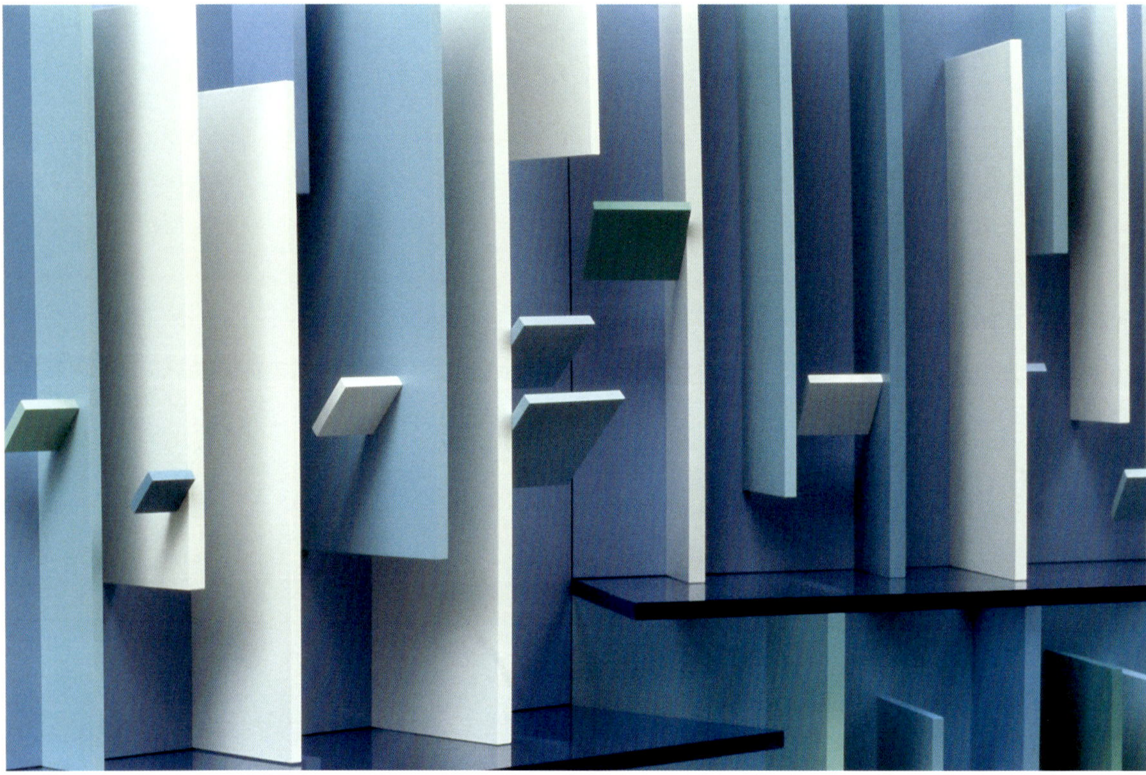

Multiplane Structurist Relief IV, No. 2 (Arctic Series), *detail* | 1987–1988
ENAMEL ON ALUMINUM AND PLEXIGLAS, 43 × 58.8 × 17.7 CM

advertising, fashion and conformity, which are the embodiment of both economic and cultural commerce.

Somehow, clarity of vision and purpose seems more attainable in the Arctic. The wildness (in Thoreau's sense) or the wilderness (in Muir's use of the word) remain the ultimate hope for our survival or preservation in revealing what is most important. It makes or allows one to see more clearly that character is the supreme beauty. True character refers to genuine essence. It is a kind of identity that is unequivocal and fundamental—neither superficial nor pretentious—and as such is surely the highest form of beauty. The Arctic still has that power of essential character that can inform and instruct us without distraction. It can reveal to us a sense of identity with the earth and all living things that modern living tends to dispel.

It all seems so clear now. But as we are quickly transported physically back to Saskatoon, I recall only too well that the Arctic clarity will not easily prevail. Yet this second Ellesmere journey reinforces my resolve that it must not easily be forgotten.

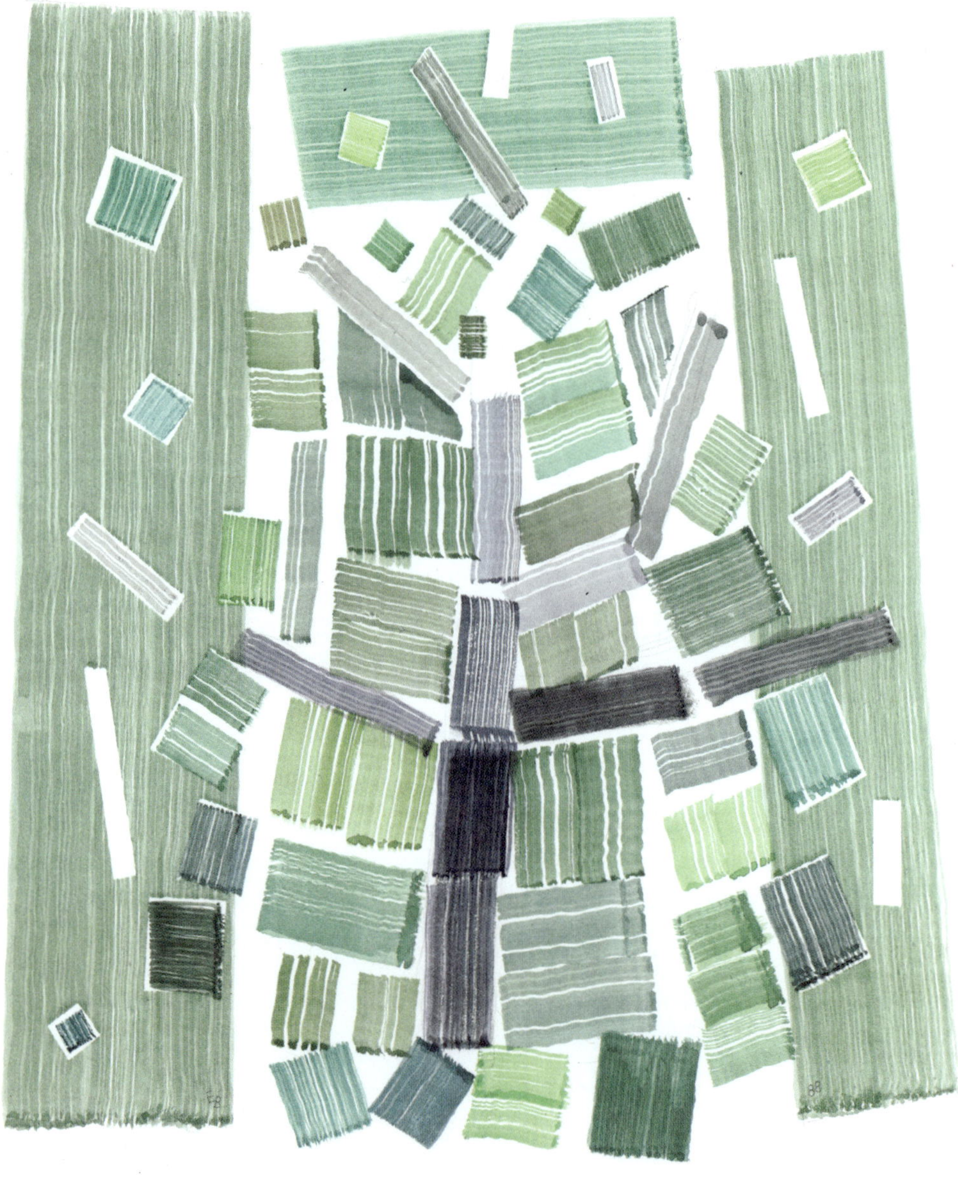

Riverbank Study No. 6 | 1989 WATERCOLOUR ON RAG BOARD, 38.1 × 31.7 CM

Poetry: An Early Interest and Initial Influence toward Abstraction

ELI BORNSTEIN

LONG BEFORE I became conscious of and interested in abstract art, I was attracted to poetry. My interest in poetry goes back to my late teens or early twenties when I first began to read literature on my own. I recall reading Rilke, his *Duino Elegies* (a book that I subsequently bound in leather and linen). Another poet was e.e. cummings whose compressed poems evoked so much with so little. In retrospect, I now realize that poetry possessed some of the abstractness that eventually developed in my art. While language itself is an abstraction of reality that evolved from the dawn of conscious communication, poetry became a further or higher level of abstraction. Poetry is a more extreme or ultimate distillation of thought, feeling and sensation concentrating essences or intensities of meaning into the most abbreviated expression. This power far exceeds that of normal conversational or written language. Poetry's power of abridgement and condensation, its elimination of anything unnecessary, is similar to those qualities found in abstract art or music. Both music and poetry preceded by centuries the modern focus upon abstract visual art.

Literal language became in poetry increasingly abstract just as mimetic, realistic, descriptive painting and sculpture became more abstract through Impressionism and Cubism. Seeing Monet, Cézanne and Brancusi in Chicago in the early 1940s in parallel with my awakening to the power of poetry enabled me to make what seemed to some a leap into abstract constructive sculpture and then low form reliefs, which evolved into abstract colour and spatial Structurist reliefs and multiplane constructions. The "leap" was actually well prepared for and more a step based upon other preceding and well-established foundations.

I remain drawn to the process of poetry. Creating a poem has an equivalence to creating abstract art, such as the editing process required to find the most fundamental or essential means or form of expression. In a word, in a sequence of words, like that of colour in art, or sound in music, or space in architecture, there can reside great concentrations and levels of meaning. Similarly, light and colour, space and structure in art inherently possess elementary powers of sensory communication akin to poetry and music.

My attraction to poetry and the poetic process have unfolded together with my interest in visual art (and from childhood an interest in classical music that surrounded me with my older sister Dorothy's daily practising as a classical pianist) as a reinforcing and interconnected kinship. Because poetry uses verbal, literal words, it may be more accessible to people than is abstract constructive art. This need not and in fact should not be so, since light and colour, space and structure are to be seen in visible nature. Yet there remain more obstacles for visual abstraction because our culture is so much more oriented to and bound together through the printed word and the photographic image.

Abstraction as a process of concentrating essences occurs intensively in poetry where single words in new associations constantly transform literal language into figurative, symbolic, metaphorical abstractions that create new kinds of perception or consciousness beyond the power or scope of literal, descriptive prose. From Shakespeare to Whitman, Frost and Stevens through Mandelstam, Brodsky and Celan, poetry creates new vision and understanding through its very abstractness.

Undoubtedly, the origins of the mechanisms of poetry are to be found in our unconscious minds. Dreams possess and utilize the very processes of poetry and art. In the dream work, as Freud demonstrated, reside the tools and methods that art and poetry employ. Imagination, invention, transformation, translation, association, inversion all occur in dreams in the most compressed or condensed form of the highest possible intensity in the briefest moment of time. One might say that art and poetry and the very process of abstraction originated in the unconscious and preceded language itself. The conscious mind has through the centuries learned, and continues to learn, how to more fully utilize these latent creative methods and processes of abstraction for our further enlightenment and awareness of the Earth and ourselves in the universe.

—Eli Bornstein
12.x.2005

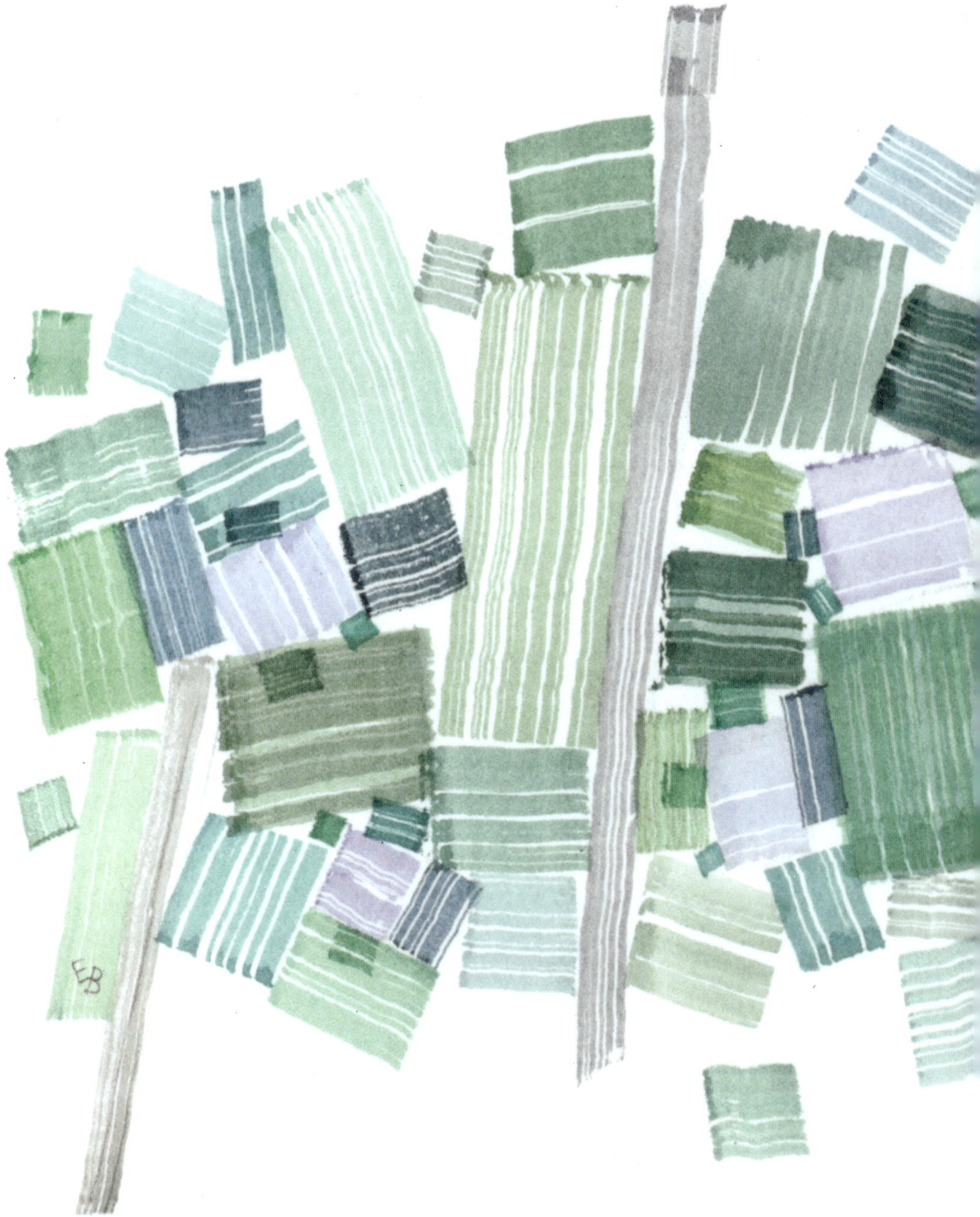

Riverbank Study No. 1 | 1989 WATERCOLOUR ON RAG BOARD, 20.3 × 24.7 CM

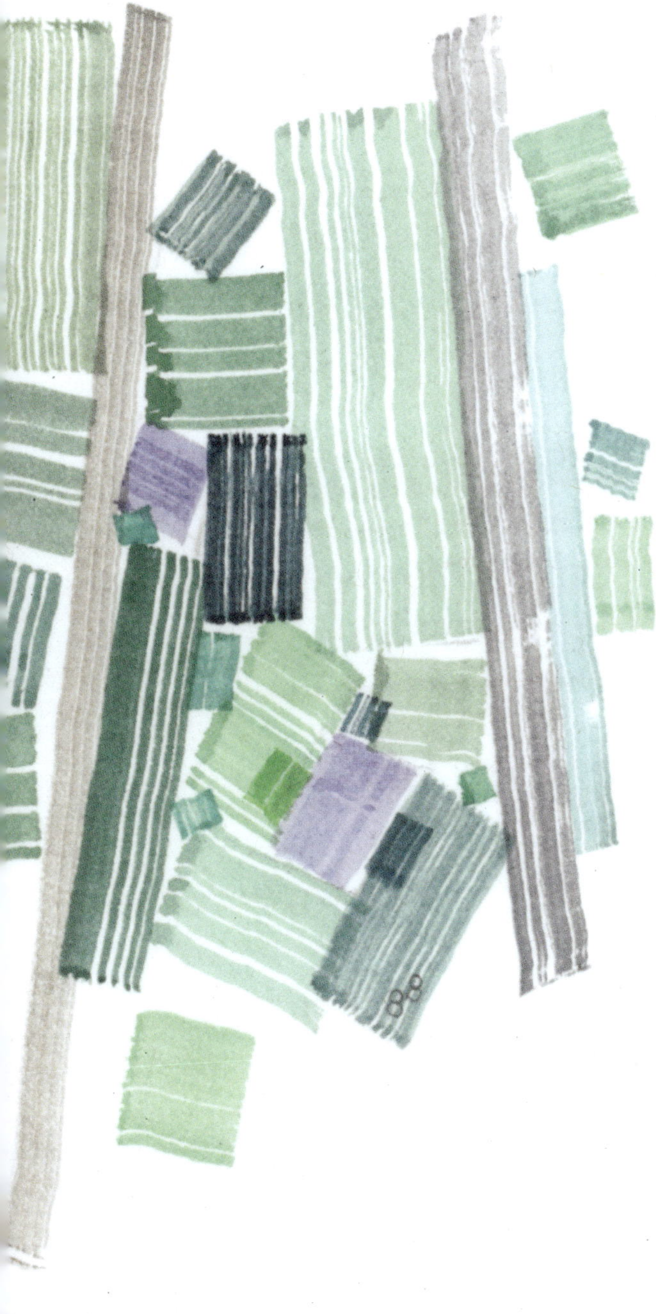

POEMS

15.IX.2001

MIGRATIONS I

Look for me among the sandhill cranes
en route to or from the Arctic in spring or fall.
Listen for their deep warble, a low chirping voice across the river.
If the sight of these cranes (or by chance it be the great blue herons)
in their majestic flight, or in their exotic, almost foreign
yet extraordinary movements and demeanour, if they
should suggest anything of me or my work, then perhaps
some momentary trace of my search for
connection between art and the universe
will have survived my journey toward infinity.

8.IV.2003

ONE TURN AT LIVING

Whatever time remaining,
you've had four score years of consciousness
and ample opportunities to act.
You've nourished needs and appetites,
savouring wondrous creations of Nature and art.
You have sought relatedness to the universe,
to find purpose and meaning in the continuity
of past, present and future
in all experiences, not least of all,
the mysteries of life and death.

You've failed more often than succeeded,
but have known unsurpassed moments
of all-consuming connectedness and illumination,
memorable sensations of wholeness
for which you are deeply thankful.

However long your turn shall be,
ending is inevitable.
You'll leave behind unfulfilled intentions,
incomplete realizations and expressions.
Eventually it will be time for first endeavours
by newborn progeny

to encounter what existence offers
in so brief a time,
generating successive singular chances
for new and diverse perceptions.

No second chance: only one turn at living
to glimpse the planetary ecology,
of which we are mere temporary reflections,
before the Earth, from which all life originates,
shall reclaim you forevermore.

2004

MIGRATIONS II

Sandhill cranes so visible, so audible in your fall migrations
with movements so leisurely yet earnest.
Far less gregarious, great blue herons
so silent and solitary in your appearances.
The gold and crimson season invites such
pleasurable pauses.
But there are hidden ironies in these brief occasions.
Seemingly unhurried, the cranes tirelessly loquacious, there is anxious
anticipation of dying days and barrenness to come.
Your flights rising effortlessly high above the river, transcending
earthly matters, are inevitably earthbound.

Art is not mere entertainment, nor idle distraction.
Vital art celebrates our connection to all migrations.
The progeny and progenitors of cranes and herons,
like our own,
form part of an endless chain of being,
before and beyond art, while yet art's deepest source.
Whoever we are, whatever we do or possess, we leave
only vanishing traces of our momentary presence,
and, like all of life, migrate infinitely toward ineffable
transfiguration.

Art remains as cumulative fossils of human creativity,
the bones of evolutionary migrations.

6.1.2005

NOW IS MORE THAN NEVER

Now is more than never.
Ever is as much as since.
How enduring is the present
as it quickly joins the past?
When the past is no longer remembered
and there are no further nows,
the future vanishes as the
present merges into never.

Consciousness is the cradle of time,
Processing past, present and future
as separate yet intermingled perceptions.
Subconscious dreams translate,
transform, and reinvent memory.
Forgetfulness erases now and ever.
Time and consciousness move inexorably
together from the beginning to the end.

Birth is time's beginning; death its end.
The gift of life is our brief window upon time.
History is the singular cumulative vision
we have of all consciousness that preceded ours.

Miraculous now momentarily glimpses
all existing ever.
Hope stands firmly on now, undaunted by never,
and persistently pursues the fragile possible future.

24.IX.2005

MIGRATION III

At summer's close, with the river low,
Our winged callers have not appeared.
Sandhill cranes usually alight nearby
on sandbars or shorelines,
their haunting warbled calls
echo across the broad river valley and
announce a brief stop en route to southern spheres.

Their voice and appearance are greatly missed.
Have they arrived and gone without notice at some early hour,
like the rising and setting sun or moon unseen,
that regularly occur, observed or not?
These movements gather days, months, years, and finally every life
into an endless all-encompassing embrace.

Seeing the great blue heron and the sandhill crane are
fleeting reminders of passing time, of the universe, and of art.
A young child, barely three, upon hearing Beethoven says
"The music makes me cry."
Is not art at its fullest, be it vocal or instrumental,
be it spectrum colours, spatial structure, gesture, or rhythm,
like Nature gazing upon or listening to its unfolding?

Crane and heron, in demeanour, standing and walking,
suggest their distant lineage, the dinosaur and Pterodactyl.
In sight and sound migration's multidimensional splendour presents
an infinity of life forming.
No despair or lamentation here. No disappointed expectations.
With modest good fortune, we rejoice in momentary conscious
connection to the sublime
singularly greatest, ultimately unfathomable, process in which
each life uniquely participates, then departs.

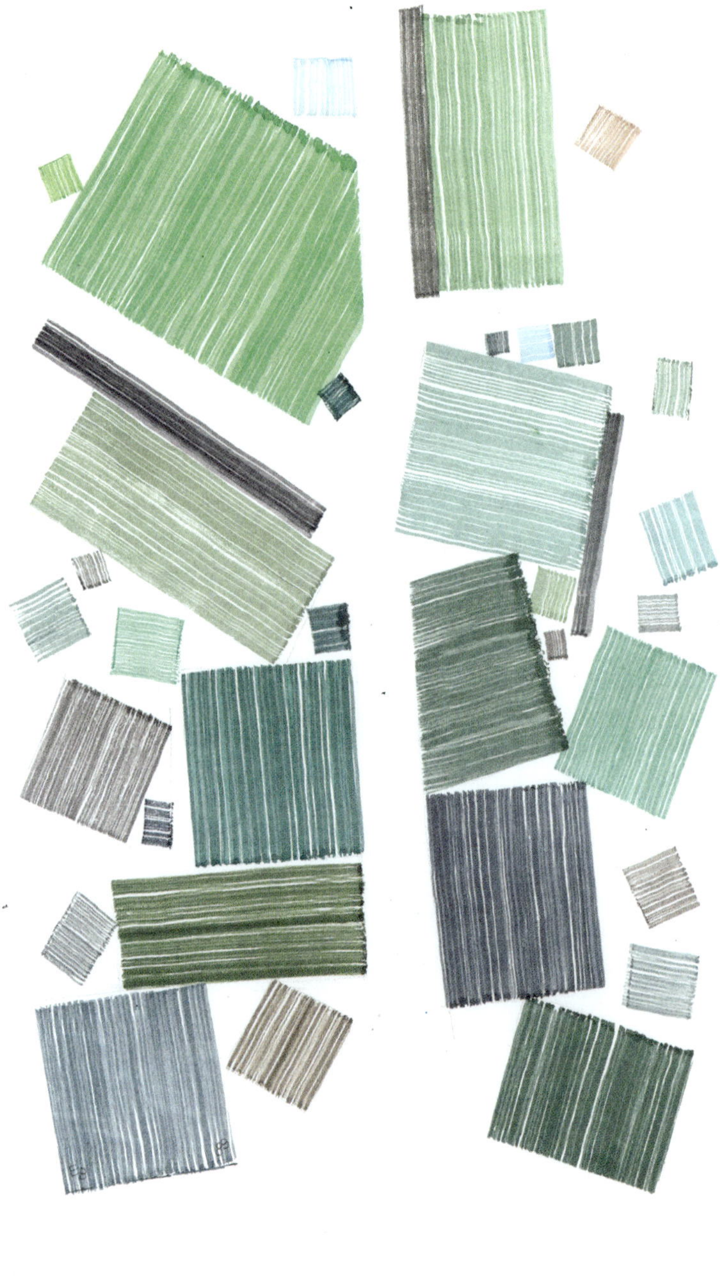

Riverbank Study No. 4 | 1989 WATERCOLOUR ON RAG BOARD, 48.0 × 39.5 CM

23.x.2006

MESSENGERS OF MIGRATION (MIGRATION IV)

Wild and garrulous sounds of Sandhill Cranes fill an
October sunrise.
Great flocks gathering on our sandbars—once
only transient islands,
now expanding presences in a shrinking river.
In our forgetfulness the great birds remind us: life and
Earth are in perpetual movement.

Warbling, screeching, croaking cries of Sandhill Cranes
reawaken ancient memory and truth.
More raucous than the turtle's voice, their call
directs our consciousness to now and forever.
The finest abstract arts displace failed religions.
Art and architecture may yet rejoin in consilient
cultural and ecological harmony.

Among all wild things, earliest source
of art and church,
a momentary glimpse of cranes or herons recalls
our alarming disconnections.
We seldom stop for migration; it always stops for us
and takes within its infinite sweep our bodies and our minds
and our hearkening to messengers.

25.X.2006

SKY TRAVELLERS

I gave my heart to the Great Blue Heron and
the Sandhill Crane,
entrusting my soul to the wildness in which the
preservation of the world abides.
We soar on the grace of wing and wind
circumnavigating Earth
above global geography in endless flight forevermore
toward infinity.

Wistfulness and joy consoled propel all life forms together
seeking universal freedom.
Sky travel unites the living and the dead in
perpetual creation and destruction.
In our passage heron and crane, ancient relatives of dinosaurs,
bind time, Earth, and sky
where regeneration unfolds in constant cosmic crossings of
rising and setting suns and moons.

12.V.2007

ILLUMINATIONS OF SPRING

Plum blossoms in a field of greens
reawaken forgotten memories.
White is the queen of colours.
Perfume stirs the sensory brain
like emanations of bridal light
softly, gently configuring profound celebration.

Twilight in May echoes profusely
fresh and delicate harmonies.
No harsh shadows.
No fierce or threatening forms;
no ominous or fearful monarch
consuming and destroying emergent radiance.

14.VI.2007

THE GREAT CONTINUUM

Dead birch trees fingering the lush riverbank
punctuate vibrant greens with grey white
gnarled gestures of death and dying.

We must recall what was alive.
Ghost-like arteries should not obscure
the living colour of today.

Making connections, cherishing the great continuum,
like memorable art through time, the remnant birch are
an indispensable presence bridging past to future.

1.X.2007

CELESTIAL DANCE

Six sandhill cranes circling high above
in a clear October sky. Hexadic choreography
with widening concentric orbits: two trios or
three duets in elliptical counter continuity becoming one sextet.
Grus canadensis move freely through the air
in perpetual harmony, defying gravity,
anticipating and surpassing human invention.

Soaring, gliding in supreme skyborne elegance contrasting
to their earthly gait, so reminiscent of reptilian origins.
Their graceful global flight lifts our spirits
with hopes for sanity to preserve biological diversity
and our brotherhood with the ancient crane.
No art, no architecture, no science or technology
performs such sublime celestial dance.

20.X.2007

A CALL TO THE PORTAL OF ETERNITY

Ancient Aboriginal and First Nations Peoples named themselves
Cranes or Echo-Makers.
The Sandhill Crane with its shrill, haunting, warbled sounds
resonating across wide dunes and stretches of prairie river bank
awakens the living to Nature's infinite entrance,
including all life and every art and architecture that was or will be.

Long before the earliest humanoid made music or dance,
the Crane circumnavigated Earth.
The Echo-Maker reminds us of our infancy
and the minimal magnitude of our movement.
The call of the Crane commands awareness of our identity, our
presence
within the grandeur of Geology and Biology, twin columns to the
portal of eternity.

4.VI.2008

IN PREPARATION

In preparation for our lifetime hence
we follow successive paths of progenitors and progeny,
yet find ourselves unprepared for final expiration
with dignity and courage before all-engulfing infinity,
unready for the physical joining of Earth and bone.

The way of flesh follows extinction of memory and hope,
love and friendship, ecstasy and despair.
Goodbye to experiencing beauty of Nature and art.
Impossible for readiness with equanimity for such loss and
the closing down of sensation and consciousness forever.

Though never fully prepared,
there is solace in brotherhood with all creations
that come into being and pass away: including
dogs and horses, herons and hawks we have seen or known.
Finally we must join the perpetual migration of all life.

In a scale of time beyond human reckoning
rivers, forests, mountains, continents and planets are in universal flux
overwhelming human life and civilizations.
In the all-connecting continuities resides the identity we seek,
Realizing our minuscule micro-moment of wondrous awareness.

26.XII.2009

ART OF THE MUSES

In Greek *mousike* means "art of the muses."
For me music is the poetry of sound
that soothes and charms and gives form to solitude.
Tireless companion, friend, devout
provider of consolation,
music is soul mate to my deepest being.

Above the current platitudes of rock and pop,
the jazz of blues and swing and cool that
move muscle and bone with joyful dance,
resides classical Elysium or Arcadia—sublime
abstraction towards which all art aspires.

Life without music is incomprehensible;
music gives rhythm and movement to the body,
offering harmony, continuity, and connectedness
to Nature and all forms and families of creation,
beyond nine sisters and planets. It adds infinite
dimensions to knowing.

3.VIII.2012

BECOMING A FLOWER

When do the leaves along a branch
terminate to become a flower?
What seeds of structure and colour
reside in the branch's end?
How does the invisible process
bring forth such focused beauty?

Becoming a flower is not unlike
the metamorphosis of a caterpillar
though flower petals don't become
wings for continental flight.
Colour and form in becoming
art seldom finds exact similitudes of Nature's processes.

Coordinated creativity or morphogenesis
occurs ubiquitously in Nature.
Becoming a human work of art can only aspire
toward such fecundity
but never achieve the birth and flight of butterflies or
a single orchid's awesome presence.

24.IX.2012

COSMIC CONTINUITY

Like exquisite plums, matured to
ripeness, that fall to Earth,
human life's end is no less a
natural termination.

Yet we fear and tremble at the
unimaginable hiatus of consciousness.

Becoming dumb, deaf,
and blind invites apprehensions beyond reason,
though human bodies like
plums have equivalence
with all creation's ends.

Despite seeming remoteness, all
living cycles are connected.

We are inexplicably ignorant of
Nature and human destiny.
If we could understand our
equivalence with all that lives,
we could identify and celebrate living and dying
as cosmic continuity.

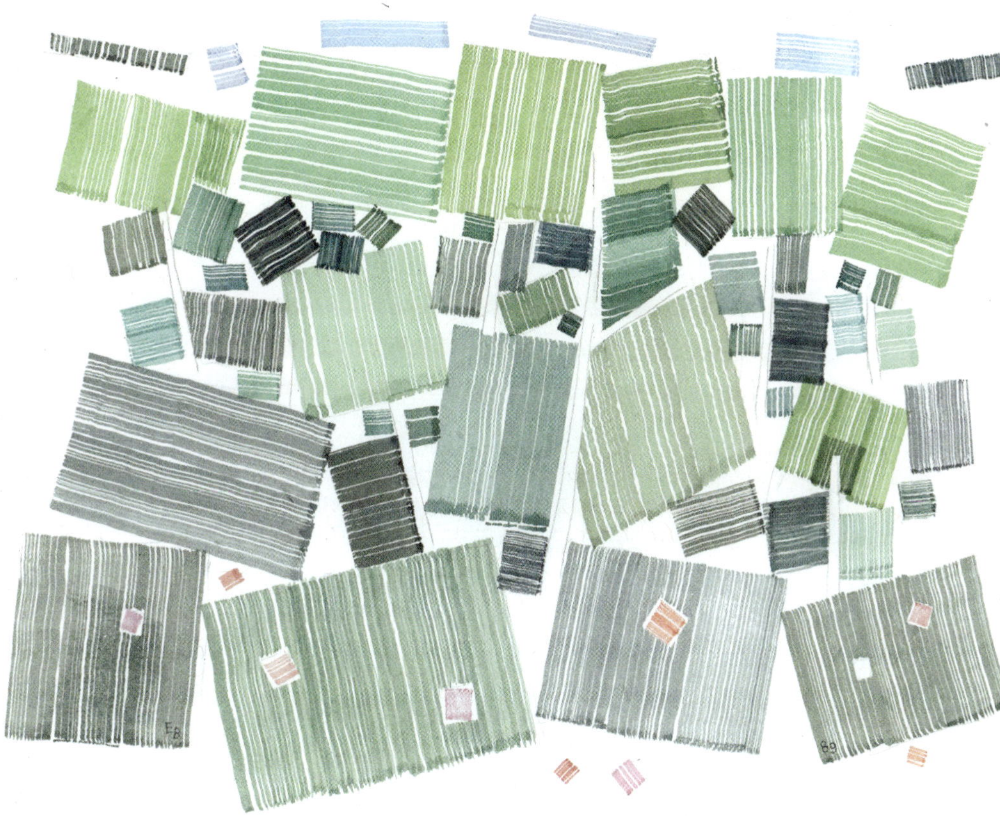

Riverbank Study No. 2 | 1989 WATERCOLOUR ON RAG BOARD, 30.5 × 40.5 CM

22.X.2012

POINTLESS PARADIGM?

All were present, as is now.
None knew why or whither hence hereafter.
Endless beauty, creativity, and mystery,
as well as profoundest tragedy prevail.

From cosmic to microcosmic creation/destruction
our "wherefores" and "whys" forevermore unanswered.
Time-bound art, music, and architecture reside
amidst infinitely evolving Nature
in all its magnificent grandeur and wild determinations.

What clear and peerless purpose have we here?
Some proclaim a sweet and happy ending.
Others who see evident truth remain doubtful of such promise.
They believe thereafter to be unknowable.
Perhaps through life-long pursuit of truth, beauty, and justice
the briefest partial sight of infinity may appear.
No specific point of view or paradigm may clearly reveal itself
in the tiny movement of consciousness through which we pass.
We may perceive life's supreme awareness of itself.

1.2013

SNOWFLAKES AND GRAINS OF SAND

Both infinite in number yet so different in form and duration.
Snowflakes are short-lived before their reformation into ice or water.
Icebergs, seas, rivers, lakes, and clouds become their eventual recycled destinations.
"No two alike" during their brief presence as exquisite and endlessly varied patterns.

Grains of sand on Earth's beaches and deserts appear through eons of gradual formation.
Their ubiquity is more selective and determined through geological means.
Their dramatic changes into sandstone or quartz require enduring extremes of pressure and heat.
The basis of glass and its preeminent transparency, silica spans the diastrophism of mountains and crystallization of jewels.

Elemental in their incomparability, snowflakes and sand express the incredible scope of Earth's creative/destructive forces.
Like varieties of art in form, structure, and expression
their separate identities connect in Nature's most fundamental processes of creativity.

18.VIII.2013

PROMISES OF REUNIONS AND CONTINUITY

Into the Earth
deeply shall I dwell
for everlasting time

with all my ancestors,
closest relatives and dearest friends,
including my beloved wife and daughters

and all my progeny and theirs.
Forgetting not my short-lived dogs:
Skippy, Brandy, Regis, Igor, Storm, and Tavish.

Then why grieve, why lament
in fear of unconsciousness and
loss of every sense?

Is it the final mockery of unfulfilled promises,
of rebirth, reunion, and continuity
that are "lost and by the wind grieved"?

No awareness of interminable habitation
residing motionless through diminishing
physical embodiment and being

toward elemental unison
with Gaia whose truest entity and scope
we humans unwisely ignore or forget.

We fail to celebrate true union
and to grieve appropriately
life's decline and end.

Our continuity prevails in Earth's
biological processes of evolution;
our ultimate destiny is geological.

Only fleeting remembrance may occur through
fragile history and culture that may
survive sufficiently to flourish briefly.

18.IX.2015

BOUNTIFUL CREATION IN ART AND NATURE

Like a bumblebee climbing up
the steep petals into opulent flowers
seeking nectar for making honey,
the artist climbs the cliffs of life experiences
manoeuvring cultural obstacles like high winds
that alter determined destinations of honeybees and hummingbirds.

Like rejection of unappreciated painting, sculpture or architecture,
interference, disruptions, disturbances
prevail for insects, animals, and artists.
Butterflies and elephants like poets and playwrights
encounter recurrent barriers
against sufficient resources for creativity or survival.
Nature's creative processes and those of art
are bound and connected in their periodic frustrations
between bountiful abundance and prolonged drought-like scarcity.

20.VIII.2016

NEVER

Never, never upon never
comes this life to me again.
Never means never forevermore
to love and be with friends and family
or see the sun and moon and stars
or feel the wetness of rain and snow,
the wind and warmth of all the weathers.
Never again to smell the perfumes of blooming flowers
nor hear talks nor sounds, nor symphonies, nor string quartets
never again to hear music or see art,
to behold and create light, colour, space or structure.
The end of living is final, is permanent.
The singularity of consciousness remains impenetrable and beyond recovery.

Biographical Notes

ROALD NASGAARD

ELI BORNSTEIN, artist, teacher, writer and publisher, was born in Milwaukee, Wisconsin, in 1922. He received a BSc in art from the Milwaukee State Teachers College in 1945. Between 1944 and 1950 he taught at the Milwaukee Art Institute and the University of Wisconsin–Milwaukee. He graduated with an MSc in fine art from the University of Wisconsin–Madison, in 1954. A visit to the IIT Institute of Design in Chicago, László Moholy-Nagy's New Bauhaus, and a period of study at the School of the Art Institute of Chicago introduced him to European Modernist tradition, while his reading of the American Transcendentalists established a foundation for his commitment to the study of nature and, later, to environmentalism.

He accepted a teaching position at the University of Saskatchewan in Saskatoon in 1950, where he was instrumental in building the Department of Art and Art History until he retired in 1990. Starting in the mid-1950s he became one of the leading practitioners of Structurist art, which evolved from his study of the Modernist tradition from Impressionism and Cézanne and through to Russian Constructivism, and Mondrian. Although he builds his Structurist reliefs using the abstract language of colour and three-dimensional geometric form, they are dedicated to the study of nature and its biological processes.

A decisive event of the mid-1950s was personally meeting the American relief artist Charles Biederman (1906–2004), the pioneer, so to speak, of nature-inflected Structurist art. Bornstein constructed his first abstract reliefs in 1957 while on sabbatical leave travelling in Europe with the specific purpose of studying Constructivism and De Stijl. Bornstein's sojourns to the Canadian Arctic in 1986 and 1987 initiated a significant formal reorientation to his work. To give voice to the North's sublimity and its silences, he learned to stretch out his reliefs into long horizontal zigzagging multiplanes with finely tuned shifts in colour gradations. This became fertile artistic territory that Bornstein would further explore back home in Saskatoon living on the panoramic banks of the South Saskatchewan River.

In 1960 he founded the internationally circulating periodical *The Structurist*, published out of the University of Saskatchewan, to which he regularly contributed art historical and theoretical essays. *The Structurist* ran for 50 years (Nos. 1–50, 1960–2010), with an anniversary issue (Nos. 51/52, 2019/2020). Over the years he has also completed major commissions for public art located in Saskatoon, Regina, Winnipeg and Bremen, Germany.

MANY OF THE PEOPLE that figure in Bornstein's Arctic travels were colleagues at the University of Saskatchewan. On his trip to Rankin Inlet in 1965 his two companions were the musician and composer Murray Adaskin and the anthropologist Robert (Bob) Williamson.

Adaskin (1906–2002) and his first wife, the soprano Frances James (1903–1988), had moved to Saskatoon in 1952 when Adaskin was appointed head of the Department of Music at the University of Saskatchewan, a position he held until 1966, after which he served as composer-in-residence until 1973. Bornstein met them shortly after their arrival, and for about a year, while a bachelor, lived with the Adaskins in their large house on University Drive. Adaskin helped make Saskatoon a major centre for the performance of contemporary Canadian music. The recordings of Inuit singing that he made during the Rankin Inlet sojourn would influence several of his compositions including *Qala and Nilaula of the North* (1969, for small orchestra), *Rankin Inlet* (1978, for piano duo) and *Eskimo Melodies* (1980, for piano).

British-born Bob Williamson (1931–2012), their host, so to speak, in Rankin Inlet, was professor of anthropology at the University of Saskatchewan, where he pioneered the university's Arctic Research and Training Centre. Born in England, he had learned Inuktitut when he lived in Pangnirtung, Nunavut, in the 1950s and founded the first Inuit language journal—*Inuktitut*. He founded the Eskimology section at the Department of Indian and Northern Affairs. In the 1960s, he served two terms as a member of the legislative council for the Northwest Territories representing the Keewatin.

BORNSTEIN'S MAJOR COLLEAGUES and encounters during the summers of 1986 and 1987 included:

Hans Siegfried Dommasch (1926–2017), Bornstein's travel companion, served as professor and head of the Department of Art and Art History at the University of Saskatchewan from 1984 to 1993; in 1975, he had established the university's first photography classes. Born in Tilsit, Germany (now in Russia), he immigrated to Canada in 1954. Needing to learn both English and an employable skill, he studied and pursued a career in photography. In 1986, he published *Prairie Giants*, a compilation of historical photographs and his own photography of prairie grain elevators. Dommasch's *Canada North of 60°*, a virtual exhibition of photographs of the people, flora, landscape and wildlife of the Canadian North (hosted online by the University of Saskatchewan Archives), draws on his several northern travels, including those with Bornstein.

James F. Basinger (b. 1951) and Bornstein became colleagues and friends when Bornstein and Dommasch investigated the Polar Continental Shelf Project (PCSP) as a means for artists to accompany scientific field parties into the Arctic. Basinger joined the faculty of the Department of Geological Sciences in the College of Arts and Science at the University of Saskatchewan in 1981. He was a seasoned Arctic explorer whose research included fossil plants and the origin and early evolution of land plants, and tertiary plants and climate change in high northern latitudes. He worked closely with Bornstein and

Dommasch to navigate their travels in the North, and in 1987 wove them into his own fieldwork on Axel Heiberg Island where, the year before, he and his colleagues made a remarkable discovery of the remains of extraordinary fossil forests that were 45 million years old. At the University of Saskatchewan, Basinger would subsequently serve as head of the Department of Geological Sciences (1997–2003), Associate Dean of Science (2004–2007), Associate Vice-President of Research (2008–2016) and, until January 2020, as Interim Vice-Provost of Faculty Relations.

In 1987 Bornstein met other distinguished scientists including Dr. Elisabeth E. McIver (1942–2001), an internationally recognized authority in the areas of paleofloristics (her husband was Jim Basinger); and Dr. Mary R. Dawson (1931–2020), a vertebrate paleontologist and curator at the Carnegie Museum of Natural History in Pittsburgh, Pennsylvania.

Bornstein's 1987 journal entries also make several references to Peter Schledermann (b. 1941), who was working in their region on Skraeling Island. Schledermann was a Dane by birth and a veteran Arctic explorer. In the early 1980s he was affiliated with the University of Calgary and was director of the Arctic Institute of North America. He did significant work on Arctic peoples, and was instrumental in the discovery of Norse artifacts among 1,000-year-old Indigenous campsites of eastern Ellesmere Island. Bornstein met him briefly while on a flying excursion when the pilot landed their helicopter on Pim Island at the camp where Schledermann and a small party were at work (18.VII.87). Schledermann's name appears a couple of days later when the American author Barry Lopez (1945–2020) was dropped off at Alexandra Fjord on his way to visit him. In 1986 Lopez, an essayist and fiction writer, had won the National Book Award for non-fiction with *Arctic Dreams* (1986)—the only book that Bornstein himself had brought on the trip, although he decided not to read it lest it interfere with his own immediate responses to the Arctic. The two spent a short but pleasant time together.

And finally, there was Barry Hough, the PCSP base manager, stationed at Resolute, whom Bornstein and Dommasch met immediately on arrival and with whom they would maintain daily mandatory morning and evening radio contact throughout their two stays. Hough was the air transport coordinator and the lifeline for the Arctic investigators, scientists and artists who were strewn over the vast Arctic territory of northern Canada.

ROALD NASGAARD is a teacher, writer and curator. The publication of *Eli Bornstein: Arctic Journals 1986 and 1987* brings together his long-standing commitments to both abstract art and landscape painting. He is the author of the critically acclaimed book *Abstract Painting in Canada*. His major exhibitions and accompanying books include *The Mystic North: Symbolist Landscape Painting in Northern Europe and North America 1890–1940*; the first Gerhard Richter retrospective in North America; *The Automatiste Revolution: Montreal 1941–1960*; and *The Plasticiens and Beyond: Montreal 1955–1970*. More recently he co-curated *Mystical Landscapes* for the Art Gallery of Ontario and the Musée d'Orsay in Paris, and *Higher States: Lawren Harris and His American Contemporaries* for the McMichael Canadian Art Collection. His book on the Montreal artist Charles Gagnon and an e-book on Eli Bornstein for the Art Canada Institute are currently forthcoming.

Acknowledgements

ROALD NASGAARD, art historian and curator, offered immeasurable guidance and due diligence, and gave constant good counsel with unlimited patience. Without him, these journals could not have been published.

Cheryl Avery, archivist for the University of Saskatchewan, used her invaluable coordinating skills and abiding resilience in her search for the best and truest reproductions of the images chosen for this publication. This project could not have come to fruition without her steadfast dedication.

Beth Matheson used her exacting eye for colour, and Troy Mamer understood the complexities of photographing Structurist reliefs.

Near the time of Jim Basinger's remarkable discovery of the remains of a 45-million-year-old fossil forest on Axel Heiberg Island, the Polar Continental Shelf Project created an opportunity for artists to explore the high Arctic. Hans Dommasch and I were given this extraordinary opportunity for an incredible journey.

Memories are stirred of my friend and colleague, Hans, who shared with me the rare privilege of the vast space, austere beauty and soul-piercing silence of our far northern lands.

My gratitude and thanks.

ELI BORNSTEIN, SASKATOON

THE IDEA FOR THIS BOOK emerged around Eli and Christina Bornstein's dining room table as we were discussing my forthcoming e-book on Eli's work for the Art Canada Institute. Eli, quite understandably, liked the idea of having a real print book, something one could hold in one's hand, and publishing his Arctic journals had been a lingering wish. Figure 1 in Vancouver, whose principals I had worked with on earlier projects, quickly became an enthusiastic publisher.

We are grateful for the generous support this project received from University of Saskatchewan President Stoicheff and acting Dean of the Library Charlene Sorenson.

This book, of course, is Eli's. But in the process of making it happen, I have been grateful to both Eli and Christina for background stories, biographical details, delightful lunches and dinners and so much more. My other indispensable partner in Saskatoon has been Cheryl Avery, archivist at the University of Saskatchewan, who has been tireless in her pursuit of the images for the book. We are grateful for the contributions and assistance of Blair Barbeau, Jim Basinger, Cathy Berg, David Bindle, Lisa Carpenter, Craig Harkema, Troy Mamer, Luke Muller, Shalini Reymond, Joel Salt, Lisa Shiffman, Norman Zepp; and, finally, to my wife Lori Walters, always a patient reader and re-reader. Without them this book could neither have been undertaken, nor completed.

ROALD NASGAARD, TORONTO

Notes

1 According to the annual report from the University of Saskatchewan Department of Art for 1964–1965: under grants in aid of research, "E. Bornstein: grant of $600 from Institute for Northern Studies to make trip to Arctic to visit Eskimo communities in order to assess their art and the possibility of setting up further research projects, May 17–May 27, 1965." Source: University of Saskatchewan Archives, RG2001.4, B-14/18, box 11.

2 University of Saskatchewan Archives, MG 216, Guide to the RG Williamson fonds.

3 Hans S. Dommasch, "Introduction," *Canada North of 60°*: digital.scaa.sk.ca/gallery/northern/dommasch/, 2002.

4 University of Saskatchewan Archives, RG2139, box 6, Bornstein, Eli.

5 According to Dommasch, "George Hobson, M.Sc., Director of the Polar Continental Shelf Project, interviewed us and found us trustworthy enough to be turned loose in the wilderness of Canada and granted fly-in support after we arrived in Resolute." Dommasch, "Introduction," *Canada North of 60°*: digital.scaa.sk.ca/gallery/northern/dommasch/, 2002.

6 Eli Bornstein, "The Color 'Molecule' in Art," *The Structurist*, No. 13/14 (1973–1974), 112–114.

7 See *"An Art at the Mercy of Light": Recent Work by Eli Bornstein* (Mendel Art Gallery in Saskatoon, 2013, curated by Oliver A.I. Botar). The exhibition features Bornstein's post-Arctic career starting in the late 1980s. See: umanitoba.ca/schools/art/media/SOA_CATALOGUE_AnArtAttheMercyofLight_EliBornstein.pdf.

8 Julian Barnes, *Keeping an Eye Open: Essays on Art* (Random House Canada, 2015), 114.

9 On his unfinished work "Hérodiade," in a letter to Henri Cazalis (30 October 1864); *Oeuvres complètes* (1945) edited by Henri Mondor and G. Jean-Aubry, p. 307, as translated in Rosemary Lloyd, *Mallarmé: The Poet and His Circle* (Cornell, 2005), 48.

10 Eli Bornstein, "Aspects of Transparency and Reflection," *The Structurist*, No. 27/28 (1987), 58–59.

11 Ralph Waldo Emerson, "Nature" (1836), in *The Selected Writings of Ralph Waldo Emerson* (Modern Library, 1992), 6.

Suggested Reading

BORNSTEIN HAS THROUGHOUT his career been a prolific writer. His critical and theoretical essays appeared regularly in the periodical *The Structurist*, which he edited and published out of the University of Saskatchewan in Saskatoon: Nos. 1–50, 1960–2010, with an anniversary issue, No. 51/52, 2019/2020.

FRITZ-JOBSE, JONNEKE, in *Eli Bornstein: Art toward Nature* (Mendel Art Gallery, 1996). Exhibition catalogue with contributions by Eli Bornstein, and a detailed list of exhibitions and bibliography up to 1996.

BOTAR, OLIVER A.I. "'The constructed relief is an art at the mercy of light,'" in *"An Art at the Mercy of Light": Recent Works by Eli Bornstein* (Mendel Art Gallery, 2013). Exhibition catalogue with contributions from Eli Bornstein and Rodney LaTourelle.

NASGAARD, ROALD. "To Invent the Truth," in *Artist in Focus: Eli Bornstein* (Remai Modern, 2019). Exhibition catalogue.

NASGAARD, ROALD. *Eli Bornstein: Life & Work* (Art Canada Institute, forthcoming).